As a bonus for purchasing this book, you're invited to take a complimentary TriMetrix EQ assessment. This custom version highlights key insights to help you grow and lead more effectively.

To claim your one-time assessment,
scan the QR code below or visit:

BuildingARockstarWorkforce.com/GetMyCode

SCAN ME

WHAT PEOPLE ARE SAYING ABOUT
BUILDING A ROCKSTAR WORKFORCE

"*Building a Rockstar Workforce* goes beyond theory—it delivers practical tools that people at every level can apply right away to elevate their impact. After putting hundreds of employees through Rockstar's training, I'm excited to share this book as a powerful resource to continue their growth and development."

—Justin Martin, CEO, Nox Group

"Simon Sinek famously said, 'Be the leader you wish you had.' *Building a Rockstar Workforce* is the roadmap to do exactly that by offering practical, clear, and built for real-world leadership growth."

—Matt Hensler, Executive Consultant, Inswing

"*Building a Rockstar Workforce* is the complete package. It draws on both personal and professional experiences, and challenges the reader with each step—each chapter—along the way. This is a must-read for anyone looking to lead more effectively at work and in life."

—Kimberly Davids, President and CEO, Arizona Builders Alliance

"If you're ready to elevate talent at every level of your organization and enhance everyone's leadership skills, this book is your roadmap. *Building a Rockstar Workforce* is not just a book, it's a transformational toolkit for building a culture of engagement, fulfillment, and impact."

—Josh Stroot, COO, ICON National

"The authors share a thoughtful process for helping employees discover and apply their strengths in the workplace—something we've experienced across multiple leadership cohorts. Their approach shifted how our leaders view their roles, leading to stronger teams and more intentional collaboration."

—Chuck English, President, Hunter Contracting

"This book is a powerful reminder that leadership isn't about your title—it's about how you show up for others. Everyone can lead, and this book shows you how."

—David Bonnstetter, CEO, TTI Success Insights

"*Building a Rockstar Workforce* is a powerful call to action that redefines leadership for the modern workplace. With practical insights and proven strategies, this book shows how empowering individuals at every level—not just those with titles—can spark a culture of accountability, engagement, and lasting success. If you're ready to unlock the full potential of your team, this is your blueprint."

—Erik Droge, CFO, Facings of America

"This book provides great guidance on leadership in the workforce. It's about showing up for your people with a genuine approach. Super practical, super relatable and just makes you want to be better."

—Chris Quigley, General Superintendent, Chasse Building Team

"I found *Building a Rockstar Workforce* to be a game changer in developing a strong, effective team. It emphasizes that leadership is not about titles but about how you serve others, demonstrating that everyone has the potential to lead."

—Carrie Rivera, COO, Burns Dentistry

"This book is a powerful reminder that great leadership begins within. It offers a transformative guide for anyone ready to lead with purpose, clarity, and impact."

—Vanessa Boettcher, Chief Operating Officer, TTI Success Insights

BUILDING A
Rockstar
WORKFORCE

Strengthen Emotional Intelligence
Enhance People Skills
and Elevate Impact
at Every Level

ADAM AND
AMBER WONG

Building a Rockstar Workforce

Strengthen Emotional Intelligence, Enhance People Skills, and Elevate Impact at Every Level

Adam and Amber Wong © 2025

Hardcover ISBN: 978-1-61206-354-6
Softcover ISBN: 978-1-61206-355-3
eBook ISBN: 978-1-61206-356-0

For more information and resources, or to book Adam or Amber to speak, visit BuildingARockstarWorkforce.com or email Adam@RockstarWorkforce.com or Amber@RockstarWorkforce.com

The following are registered trademarks of TTI Success Insights, Ltd. Any use must acknowledge ownership by TTI Success Insights, Ltd.: 12 Driving Forces®, Emotional Quotient™, Motivation Insights®, TTI Success Insights®, TriMetrixEQ®, and TriMetrix®.

Produced in partnership with TTI Success Insights.

Published by

aloha
PUBLISHING

AlohaPublishing.com

Printed in the United States

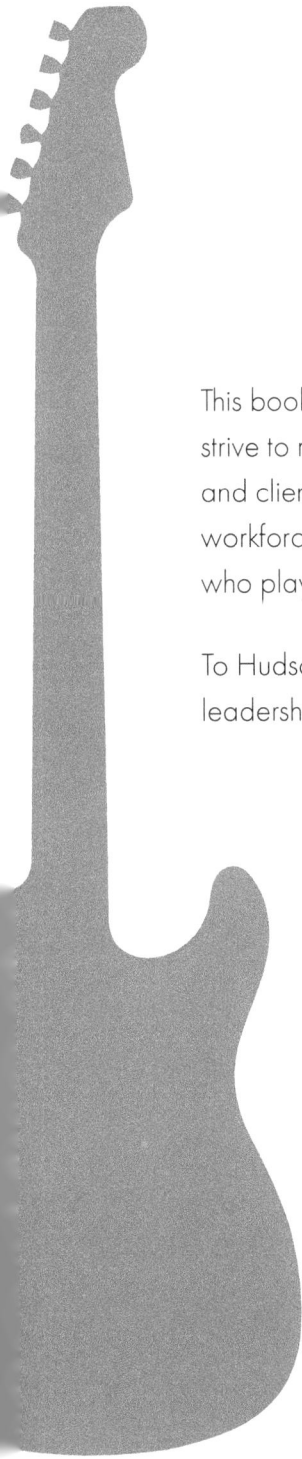

Dedication

This book is a tribute to those who invest in growth—leaders who strive to make a difference, teams who embrace the challenge, and clients who trust us to help shape their culture. Rockstar workforces aren't built alone, and we are grateful for everyone who plays a part in elevating others.

To Hudson and Harper, whose curiosity and joy remind us why leadership begins at home—you inspire us every day.

Contents

Introduction
The Mindset Behind a Rockstar Workforce

What if leadership wasn't about a title but about creating real impact? For decades, businesses have equated leadership with management, assuming that authority, titles, and tenure define who leads. But in today's fast-paced and ever-changing world, this outdated mindset holds organizations back. Leadership isn't just for executives—it must exist at all levels of an organization. The success of a business depends on its people, and the most effective organizations empower every individual to step into leading, regardless of title.

WHY LEADERSHIP MUST EXIST AT EVERY LEVEL

Think about the best workplaces you've experienced. They aren't just made up of strong executives; they thrive because they develop leaders at every level. Leadership is about action, not position. When companies invest in growing leadership skills across their workforce, they create a culture of accountability, innovation, and high performance.

At Rockstar Workforce, we've spent years working with businesses to elevate talent for everyone from the receptionist to the boardroom. Companies that invest in developing everyone have seen measurable results—higher employee Net Promoter Scores (eNPS), increased employee engagement, and recognition as Best Places to Work.

eNPS is a key metric that measures how likely employees are to recommend their organization as a great place to work. A high eNPS score reflects strong employee satisfaction, loyalty, and a workplace culture where people feel valued and engaged.

COMPANIES WITH STRONG ENPS SCORES NOT ONLY RETAIN TOP PERFORMERS BUT ALSO ATTRACT HIGH-CALIBER TALENT LOOKING FOR AN EXCEPTIONAL WORK ENVIRONMENT.

Beyond internal improvements, these organizations foster a culture where people thrive, creating a ripple effect that drives innovation and long-term success. We've seen firsthand how developing everyone transforms lives, teams, and businesses—and this book is your guide to making that transformation happen.

THE JOURNEY TO ROCKSTAR WORKFORCE

Our leadership journey didn't start in a boardroom. We launched Rockstar Workforce with the goal of helping businesses hire the right people and develop leaders. In the early years, we primarily focused on development programs for mid- to senior-level managers. Then, a few forward-thinking companies asked us to work with employees across all levels of their organizations. That's when it clicked—we saw the transformative power of leadership development when applied to everyone, not just managers. It became clear that this approach could unlock untapped potential in individuals and drive lasting success for organizations. We've seen this happen firsthand with our clients, who have cultivated vibrant workplace cultures, achieved their growth goals, and consistently ranked among or aspired to be on the Best Places to Work list year after year. We don't think it's a coincidence that people love working in a place where they feel valued and important.

Now, we're on a mission to reshape how leadership is viewed. The idea that leadership training is only for managers is outdated, and we're working to change that mindset. Leadership skills—communication, accountability, problem-solving, and emotional intelligence—are valuable for everyone. Whether someone is an entry-level employee or a senior executive, these skills empower them to lead from wherever they are. Our goal is to make this shift widespread, helping organizations embrace leadership development as a core part of their culture and a catalyst for growth.

A TALE OF TWO EMPLOYEES

Imagine two employees facing the same workplace challenge—a breakdown in communication between departments, causing project delays.

Alex, a frontline employee with no formal leadership training, is frustrated. He avoids confrontation and assumes it's management's responsibility to fix the issue. He complains to his colleagues, but nothing changes. His motivation declines, and his team feels stuck in the same cycle.

Jordan, on the other hand, has built skills in communication, emotional intelligence, and problem-solving. Instead of waiting for someone else to act, Jordan takes initiative. She reaches out to the other department, asks clarifying questions, and uses active listening to uncover the root cause. She then proposes a simple process change that eliminates the delay. Leadership notices, and within a few months, Jordan is recognized for problem-solving and given new opportunities for growth.

This is the difference that leadership skills make—not just at the executive or mid-management level, but in everyday situations where proactive employees create impact. By developing these skills, individuals, teams, and organizations thrive.

CHANGING THE MINDSET ON LEADERSHIP

Skepticism around leadership development for all employees is common. Many assume leadership skills are only relevant for those with formal management responsibilities. However, the reality is that leadership is not about titles—it's about influence, problem-solving, and the ability to drive positive change. Organizations that empower employees at all levels to take ownership and actively contribute create company cultures of collaboration, innovation, and engagement—ultimately creating a rockstar workforce that propels success from the ground up.

OUR WORK AND THE FOUNDATIONS PROGRAM

At Rockstar Workforce, our three-part leadership development program is designed to cultivate leadership capabilities at every level. The first and most critical part of that program is Rockstar Foundations, which helps individuals master interpersonal communication, enhance emotional intelligence, and navigate conflict effectively. This book is built on the core pillars of our Foundations program:

1. **Personal Leadership Profile** – Understanding your strengths, communication style, and leadership tendencies.

2. **Dynamic Communication** – Learning how to adapt communication to build relationships and lead effectively.

3. **Emotional Intelligence** – Developing self-awareness, self-regulation, and the ability to understand others.

4. **Managing Conflict** – Navigating difficult conversations and turning conflict into a tool for growth.

Each of these elements plays a crucial role in developing leadership skills that make a tangible difference, not only in careers and organizational success but also in building essential life skills that enhance personal relationships and daily interactions.

WHAT YOU'LL GAIN FROM THIS BOOK

This book goes beyond theory; it offers a hands-on guide filled with actionable strategies designed to meet you where you are, whether you're an executive making strategic decisions, a manager guiding a team, or an individual contributor striving to grow. No matter your role, leadership encompasses many facets: building relationships, fostering trust, communicating effectively, influencing others, problem-solving, and driving positive change. Here's what you can expect to gain:

- A deeper understanding of your own leadership strengths and areas for growth

- Practical tools to enhance communication and collaboration

- Strategies to develop emotional intelligence and manage stress effectively

- Techniques to handle conflict productively and build a stronger workplace culture

- **Objective, personalized feedback through a TriMetrix EQ® custom assessment** from TTI Success Insights®, so you can apply the results as you learn: find your unique code on the first page of the book

You'll also find digital resources and tools to help you apply these lessons in real time. You can access these resources at BuildingARockstarWorkforce.com.

THE KEY TO BUILDING ROCKSTARS: ACTION ITEMS

As you begin this journey, we challenge you to commit to your own leadership growth. At the end of each chapter, you'll find a list of intentional and targeted **action items** designed to help you get the most out of this experience. After all, leadership isn't a talent you're born with—it's a skill you develop. And like any skill, the more you practice, the better you get.

In Chapter 1, we'll explore one of the most powerful shifts a company can make: developing leadership skills at every level of the organization. You'll discover how investing in your people, regardless of title, can transform your culture, boost engagement, and drive real results.

Let's dive in!

BuildingARockstarWorkforce.com

Elevating Talent at Every Level

A REAL EXAMPLE OF ELEVATING TALENT AT EVERY LEVEL: RICHARD AND ERIK

Richard and Erik, the owners of a Phoenix-based family-run business, always believed in investing in their people. For several years, they sent one or two managers to our year-long public leadership program, where they gained valuable skills that helped them grow professionally and lead more effectively. Richard and Erik were impressed with their transformation and saw the positive impact on the company's culture and operations.

But then the two had a realization: if investing in leadership training for just a few managers produced these results, what would happen if they developed everyone in the company?

After a few years of selectively sending managers through the program, they approached us with a bold request—to design a leadership development program for every single person in their company. This meant developing not just managers but also frontline employees, new interns, administrative staff, and even senior executives.

For the past three years (and counting), we have met with their entire company every quarter for a half-day offsite training, refining their leadership and interpersonal skills—skills that every employee, in every role, can apply daily.

THE IMPACT?

The results speak for themselves:

- **Increased organizational vision**: Everyone in the company now understands and is aligned with the bigger picture.

- **Stronger collaboration**: Employees work together more effectively, bridging gaps between departments and roles.

- **Commitment to strategy and goals**: With shared leadership principles, people take greater ownership of their contributions.

- **A willingness to engage in healthy conflict**: Team members no longer shy away from tough conversations but embrace them productively.

- **A huge increase in eNPS (employee Net Promoter Score)**: Employees feel valued, heard, and empowered.

- **Recognition as a "Best Place to Work"**: The company consistently earns high marks for its engaging and supportive workplace culture.

Richard and Erik's story demonstrates why leadership isn't just for managers—it's for everyone. When companies elevate talent for every employee, they unlock the full potential of their workforce and create a culture where people want to stay, contribute, and grow.

THE CASE FOR ELEVATING TALENT AT EVERY LEVEL

Leadership is not defined by titles or authority. It's defined by the ability to positively influence others, solve problems, and take ownership in any role. Investing in talent across an entire company creates a workforce that is not only more engaged but also more adaptable and innovative.

TRUE, EFFECTIVE LEADERSHIP IS LESS ABOUT HIERARCHY AND MORE ABOUT THE ABILITY TO INFLUENCE, COLLABORATE, AND PROBLEM-SOLVE—SKILLS THAT ARE CRUCIAL IN ANY ROLE.

Organizations that focus on talent development experience tangible benefits. Research consistently shows that companies with development programs see improvements in employee engagement, retention, and overall performance. Employees who feel invested in their growth are more likely to stay and make meaningful contributions, driving the long-term success of their organizations.

INVESTING IN PEOPLE FOR LONG-TERM SUCCESS: JUSTIN

Justin, a highly respected leader in the construction industry, has always been a strong believer in personal and professional growth. Early on, he invested in coaching, mentorship, and formal training for his executive team, helping them grow as leaders. While this approach strengthened his senior team, his company was expanding rapidly and he soon faced a new challenge—his business was growing faster than he could develop new leaders.

At the same time, many of his most experienced employees were near retirement, taking years of industry expertise with them. Justin recognized that to sustain growth and maintain a strong culture, leadership couldn't just be a skill set for executives—it needed to be part of every role in the company.

That's when he took a broader approach. Instead of limiting leadership development to just the executive team, Justin expanded training to include every employee, from early-career professionals to supervisors to managers of managers.

THE IMPACT? A STRONGER, MORE ADAPTABLE WORKFORCE

Since building leadership skills became a companywide priority, Justin's business has experienced tremendous growth, expanding into new markets and multiple regions. His workforce has more than quadrupled, and his company continues to be recognized for its strong culture and employee loyalty.

By making leadership accessible to everyone, Justin has built a company where people develop, stay, and contribute at a higher level—which reinforces a culture of growth, adaptability, and innovation.

THE SCIENCE BEHIND DEVELOPING TALENT

Before founding Rockstar Workforce, we spent years at TTI Success Insights®, a global leader in behavioral science and talent assessments. Adam spent seven years there, ultimately serving as Senior Vice President, while Amber also played a key role in the Professional Business Services Division.

> OUR WORK AT TTI TAUGHT US ONE FOUNDATIONAL TRUTH: SELF-AWARENESS IS THE FIRST STEP TOWARD GROWTH.

Today, we remain closely connected to TTI as members of their Saguaro Group, a select advisory team that helps shape the future of leadership assessments. Our experiences in developing and refining these tools reinforced what we now teach—understanding your own behaviors, motivations, and emotions is crucial to personal and professional success.

WHY LEADERSHIP ASSESSMENTS MATTER

One of the most powerful tools we use is the TriMetrix EQ® assessment, which provides insights into an individual's strengths, blind spots, and leadership potential.

TriMetrix EQ uniquely integrates three sciences—Behaviors (DISC), 12 Driving Forces®, and Emotional Quotient™ (EQ) or emotional intelligence—to create a comprehensive understanding of how a person acts, why they take action, and how well they manage emotions in their interactions.

- 🛡 **Behaviors (DISC)** – How an individual prefers to act and interact in various situations (chapter 3).

- 🛡 **12 Driving Forces®** – What motivates an individual and why they take action (chapter 4).

- 🛡 **Emotional Quotient™ (EQ)** – How well they understand and regulate emotions in themselves and others (chapters 8 and 9).

People often react the same way when they receive their report: "Wow, this is so accurate and brutally honest. It validates things I know about myself—even the things I don't like. It hits differently when you read it about yourself." The reason is simple—we all have patterns of behavior that we may not fully recognize until they are reflected back at us.

Beyond self-awareness, this report provides a framework for growth in areas like communication, decision-making, and emotional intelligence. After working with thousands of individuals, we can confidently say that the insights found in TriMetrix EQ are some of the most impactful we've encountered in leadership development.

In addition to the assessments, we also introduce the concept of leadership skills with a list of 25 skills or competencies. Awareness of these skills can help people recognize more of their strengths and, with an understanding of the ones most critical to success, add goals for improvement where needed for those most important abilities. These skills are introduced in chapter 5.

HOW TRIMETRIX EQ TRANSFORMED MY LEADERSHIP (ADAM)

Before I truly understood myself, I led others the way I had been taught and observed others doing—through a matter-of-fact, old-school approach of managing down. I focused on directing and controlling outcomes rather than developing and empowering people. At the time, I thought I was leading effectively, but in reality, I was getting in my own way.

It wasn't until I took the TriMetrix EQ assessment and engaged in a variety of leadership development experiences that I realized how much my own behaviors, motivators, and emotional intelligence impacted the people around me. The insights from my report were eye-opening. It was brutally honest, showcasing both the strengths I leaned on and the blind spots I had been avoiding.

> THIS NEWFOUND SELF-AWARENESS DIDN'T JUST CHANGE HOW
> I LED AT WORK—IT RESHAPED EVERY PART OF MY LIFE.

It helped me connect more deeply with Amber (my wife), become a more effective senior leader overseeing a team of high performers, and later on, navigate my roles as a coach, mentor, business owner, and father.

I wish I had been introduced to this sooner. It wasn't until I was in my late 20s that I discovered these insights. Looking back, I can't help but wonder how much this understanding could have helped me navigate challenges earlier in life, my career, and those first management positions. This realization is one of the main reasons we are writing this book—to give others access to these insights earlier in their journeys.

HOW TO GET THE MOST FROM THIS BOOK

This book is meant to be more than something you simply read. Its purpose is to prompt action. Your purchase of this book includes a complimentary TriMetrix EQ assessment, designed to highlight the most essential insights to guide your development. This custom version of the TriMetrix EQ was created specifically for readers of this book. Chapters in this book will guide you through different sections of your report, helping you interpret and apply the insights in a meaningful way. Throughout the book, you'll explore how your behaviors, driving forces, and emotional intelligence impact your leadership style and daily interactions.

To claim your one-time assessment, scan the QR code on the first page of this book or visit BuildingARockstarWorkforce.com/GetMyCode

Your report will serve as a personalized guide throughout this book, helping you apply the insights directly to your development.

Additionally, we've developed supplementary exercises that align with your report, which can also be found on the book's website, BuildingARockstarWorkforce.com. These exercises will allow you to deepen your understanding and put your learning into practice in real time.

Chapter 1 Action Items

1. **Take your TriMetrix EQ assessment** by scanning the QR code on page 1 of the book or visiting BuildingARockstarWorkforce.com/GetMyCode and following the instructions. Use your assessment results as a guide throughout this book.

2. **Review your TriMetrix EQ report**, paying attention to both strengths and blind spots, and reflect on how they impact your interactions and leadership approach. We will continue to re-visit your report as you progress further through this book.

3. **Explore the book's additional resources** at BuildingARockstarWorkforce.com to access supplementary exercises designed to help you deepen your understanding and apply your TriMetrix EQ results in real-world scenarios.

4. **Commit to one action** based on what you've learned in this chapter. Identify one specific action step you will take this week to elevate your leadership, communication, or self-awareness.

5. **Track your progress** by keeping a simple journal or note on your phone where you document small wins and insights related to your growth. Regular reflection will help reinforce your development over time.

2

Self-Awareness Isn't Optional:
It's Your Superpower

Self-awareness is a cornerstone of personal and professional growth. It involves understanding many aspects of yourself, your life, and your work. As we explore tools like the DISC assessment, emotional intelligence, and driving forces, self-awareness becomes about recognizing how you prefer to work and communicate.

MOST IMPORTANTLY, SELF-AWARENESS IS ABOUT BEING AWARE OF HOW YOU COME ACROSS TO OTHERS AND WHAT ADJUSTMENTS YOU CAN MAKE TO ENHANCE YOUR INTERACTIONS.

A deep understanding of personal strengths and blind spots is essential when developing yourself and others. Whether you are managing a team or focusing on your own growth, the first step is to better understand yourself. We're going to break this down into four important areas:

- 🎸 Uncover your strengths and blind spots.

- 🎸 Learn how to maximize your leadership style.

- 🎸 Understand how your approach impacts others.

- 🎸 Create your personal development plan.

WHY YOU NEED TO KNOW YOUR BEHAVIORAL STYLE AND STRENGTHS

Many people don't fully realize how their communication and behavioral styles shape their interactions and relationships, both at work and in their personal lives. The DISC assessment provides a clear framework to understand your unique style, including how you communicate and interact with others. It will help you evaluate your strengths and blind spots, offering insights into how you prefer to communicate and work, and why you excel in certain roles.

Understanding your strengths allows you to identify what you excel at and how to leverage those abilities effectively. By focusing on these strengths, you can achieve greater success in your current role and shape the direction of your career.

PEOPLE THRIVE WHEN THEY FOCUS ON WHAT THEY DO BEST.

Identifying key strengths can be challenging for many people. We often go through our daily routines without stopping to reflect on what we naturally do well. Sometimes, strengths feel so second nature that we overlook them entirely, assuming they're not special or unique. Other times, we focus so much on areas of improvement that we fail to recognize where we already excel. This is why seeking feedback from others, reflecting on past successes, and paying attention to tasks that energize us can be invaluable in uncovering our core strengths.

REFLECTIVE QUESTION: WHAT ARE THREE STRENGTHS YOU CONSISTENTLY RELY ON, AND HOW DO THEY IMPACT YOU?

If you're struggling to pinpoint your strengths, consider moments when you felt most confident, accomplished, or engaged. What were you doing in those situations? What kind of feedback have you received from peers, mentors, or supervisors about what you bring to the table? Strengths are often revealed in how others perceive our contributions, so gathering outside perspectives can provide important clarity.

UNDERSTANDING YOUR BLIND SPOTS

Understanding your blind spots is just as important, if not more important, than knowing your strengths. Whether you're collaborating with others, managing a team, or focusing on your personal growth, recognizing areas where you need support can help you build stronger partnerships, improve outcomes, and focus on tasks that energize you.

Blind spots are behaviors or tendencies that we may not fully recognize or actively avoid considering. Some blind spots highlight opportunities for growth—areas where developing new skills or adjusting behaviors can enhance our effectiveness. Others may reveal untapped strengths—hidden talents that when recognized can be leveraged for greater success. Just like a great mentor, assessments provide objective insights, helping to bring these hidden strengths to light so they can be nurtured and applied effectively.

Without a clear understanding of your strengths and blind spots, it's challenging to approach tasks effectively or maximize your potential. Gaining clear, actionable feedback is the foundation for building self-awareness. When you have clarity about how you work and where your strengths lie, it becomes much easier to identify the best approaches to achieve your goals.

PERSONAL STORY: USING THE 360-FEEDBACK PROCESS TO IDENTIFY BLIND SPOTS (ADAM)

Early in my career, I considered myself a highly effective leader. I focused on efficiency, meeting deadlines, and making sure tasks were completed at the highest standard. I prided myself on my ability to get things done. So, when I participated in a 360-feedback process, I assumed I would receive feedback on my strong work ethic and leadership abilities—and I did.

For the most part, the feedback was overwhelmingly positive. My team appreciated my dedication, practical thinking, and problem-solving skills. But then, a few unexpected comments caught me off guard. A couple of team members mentioned that while they respected my work, they often felt disconnected from me. I spent most of my time in my office, focused on my task list and hopping from meeting to meeting, rather than engaging with them.

This was a wake-up call. I had always assumed that my door was open—that people knew if they needed me, they could come in. But the truth was, I wasn't making myself as approachable or available as I thought.

I remembered a concept I had learned in my MBA program: **MBWA**, or **managing by walking around**. This idea was a simple but powerful reminder that while results matter, leadership is ultimately built on relationships.

Determined to change, I started spending more time outside my office. I made an effort to check in with my team, not just about work but about them as individuals. I asked about their challenges, their wins, and their ideas.

The difference was immediate. Engagement improved, collaboration increased, and morale soared. This experience reinforced a powerful lesson: self-awareness means more than knowing your strengths and weaknesses—it's also understanding how your actions impact those around you.

Even with the best intentions, we don't always see the full effect of our behaviors until we seek honest feedback and reflect on it. While I had always prided myself on efficiency and productivity, I realized that prioritizing relationships and staying engaged with my team had a far greater impact than simply managing tasks. I started making small adjustments by getting out of my office more, being intentional in my interactions, and fostering deeper connections. I not only improved morale but also strengthened collaboration. This is the essence of self-awareness: recognizing where we can improve and taking action to create meaningful change.

USING FEEDBACK TO GROW

Receiving feedback, especially unexpected feedback, can be a powerful yet uncomfortable experience.

MANY PEOPLE ASSUME THEY ARE SELF-AWARE, BUT TRUE SELF-AWARENESS OFTEN COMES FROM HOW OTHERS PERCEIVE US.

Sometimes feedback highlights strengths we don't even recognize in ourselves, and other times it reveals blind spots we didn't realize existed.

There are multiple ways to gather feedback:

- ✎ **Direct conversations** – Asking mentors, colleagues, or peers for honest input about how you show up in different situations.

- ✎ **Observation** – Paying attention to patterns in how others respond to you, both positively and negatively.

- ✎ **Self-reflection** – Looking at moments when you felt confident or challenged and assessing what contributed to those experiences.

- ✎ **Assessments and structured tools** – Providing unbiased insights into your strengths, communication style, and areas for growth.

Each of these methods can provide valuable insight into how you interact with others and where opportunities for growth may lie.

REFLECTIVE QUESTION: WHEN WAS THE LAST TIME YOU RECEIVED FEEDBACK THAT SURPRISED YOU AND HOW DID YOU RESPOND?

If reflecting on this question feels difficult, you're not alone. Many people struggle to process feedback, especially when it challenges their self-perceptions. However, feedback—whether from others or through structured assessments—offers a roadmap for growth. The TriMetrix EQ Coaching Report provides an in-depth look and offers objective insights that help you recognize patterns you may not have noticed before.

By combining real-world feedback with assessment-based insights, you gain a more well-rounded understanding of yourself. This level of self-awareness allows you to be more intentional about how you engage with others, leverage your strengths, and address areas for improvement. Now, let's explore how understanding your behavioral style and motivations can further enhance your interactions.

UNDERSTANDING PEOPLE'S BEHAVIORAL STYLES HELPS YOU LEARN TO ADAPT

Realizing how your behavior impacts others is an important part of both personal and professional growth. Every behavioral tendency has its advantages and drawbacks, depending on the situation. For instance, individuals with high D (dominance) scores on the DISC assessment often excel at making quick decisions and driving progress, but this can sometimes lead to overlooking the perspectives of those with a more reflective approach. Many participants in our programs have shared that they've learned to slow down, listen more, and create space for others to contribute. This adjustment is particularly valuable for those with a high D score in the DISC assessment, as it fosters better collaboration and more balanced outcomes. Chapter 3 will describe more about DISC.

Being aware of how others communicate is just as important as understanding your own style. Not everyone expresses their thoughts or opinions in the same way. Some individuals naturally speak up and assert their ideas, while others are more reserved and prefer to contribute in a collaborative setting. If someone isn't sharing their perspective, it doesn't mean they don't have valuable insights—it may simply mean they need a different kind of invitation to engage.

RECOGNIZING THESE COMMUNICATION STYLE DIFFERENCES ALLOWS YOU TO BE MORE INTENTIONAL ABOUT CREATING AN ENVIRONMENT WHERE ALL VOICES ARE HEARD, STRENGTHENING YOUR RELATIONSHIPS AND FOSTERING BETTER TEAMWORK.

Imagine a typical team meeting where several individuals are gathered to discuss a new project. As the discussion unfolds, the more outspoken team members naturally take the lead, sharing their ideas and driving the conversation forward. Their energy and enthusiasm set the tone, but they inadvertently dominate the discussion. Meanwhile, some quieter individuals hold back, hesitant to contribute. They may feel less comfortable speaking up in a group setting or worry that their ideas won't be well received.

In this scenario, both groups have opportunities to grow. For the more vocal participants, it's important to be intentional about involving everyone in the conversation. This could mean pausing to ask quieter colleagues for their thoughts or ensuring that the discussion remains collaborative rather than competitive. On the other hand, quieter team members can use this as a chance to practice their influence skills by speaking up and sharing their perspectives, even if it feels challenging. Each person's voice adds value, and fostering this kind of balanced dialogue strengthens the team as a whole.

Take a moment to reflect on your own experiences in group discussions. Have you ever found yourself in a situation where certain voices dominated the conversation while others remained silent? Think about the teams, meetings, or even personal interactions you've been part of. Were there moments when you could have encouraged someone to share their perspective, or times when you hesitated to speak up yourself? Recognizing these dynamics in your everyday interactions— whether at work, in social settings, or even at home—can help you become more intentional about fostering balanced conversations. By increasing your awareness of these situations, you can take small but meaningful steps to create environments where every voice is valued.

HOW DRIVING FORCES SHAPE YOUR DECISIONS

Driving forces—or motivations—provide insight into why you make decisions, whether in your personal life, at work, or elsewhere. Your primary motivations influence the choices you make, the priorities you set, and the tasks you choose to focus on first.

When your tasks and priorities align with your primary driving forces, you often experience a deeper sense of satisfaction and fulfillment. This alignment allows you to feel more engaged, energized, and motivated because you are working in ways that resonate with what you value most. Whether it's solving a challenging problem, fostering connections, or creating something innovative, aligning with your driving forces amplifies both productivity and personal contentment.

PERSONAL STORY: HOW OUR DRIVING FORCES LED TO ROCKSTAR WORKFORCE

In 2017, Amber and I were deeply motivated to create the financial security that neither of us experienced growing up. Starting our own business gave us the chance to align our goals with our core values. For me (Adam), my top three driving forces, as defined by TTI's 12 Driving Forces assessment, are *resourceful, commanding*, and *receptive*. Being resourceful drives my focus on maximizing efficiency and achieving tangible results, which a business of our own could provide. Commanding reflects my desire for autonomy and to chart my own course, while receptiveness fuels my passion for innovation and trying new approaches.

Amber's strongest driving force is also *resourceful*—she values practical outcomes and financial stability, which made our decision to start a business together deeply fulfilling. Leaving behind stable six-figure salaries was a risk, but the opportunity to pursue work in alignment with our driving forces was worth it.

As we considered this major life change, our driving forces became a framework for meaningful conversations. We openly discussed what mattered most to us and how each of our motivations would shape our decisions. For instance, I had to recognize that my love of innovation and change might clash with Amber's preference for proven methods. By understanding these differences, we were able to navigate potential conflicts and build a plan that considered both of our values. This clarity made our decision to start the business not just a leap of faith but a deliberate step toward a shared vision.

Reflecting on this experience, Amber and I realized how valuable it was to understand not just our motivations but also how they influenced our behaviors and decisions. Tools like the DISC assessment and Driving Forces framework help to uncover these deeper insights, making it easier to navigate both personal and professional growth.

UNLOCK INSIGHTS WITH YOUR TRIMETRIX EQ COACHING REPORT

If you haven't already completed the TriMetrix EQ Coaching Report, now is the time to do so. Your unique access code and instructions are on the first page of the book. This assessment provides deeper insight into your behavioral style, motivations, and emotional intelligence—key components of self-awareness. While external feedback from colleagues and mentors is valuable, structured assessments help uncover patterns you might not recognize on your own. Understanding these insights will allow you to be more intentional about how you develop your strengths and navigate challenges.

Self-awareness is an ongoing journey. The more you understand about yourself—how you communicate, what drives you, and how you interact with others—the more effectively you can grow and lead in all aspects of life. As we move forward, we'll explore how these insights influence the way you connect with and impact those around you.

Chapter 2 Action Items

1. **Ask three trusted people for feedback** on your strengths and blind spots. Gathering external feedback provides valuable insights that you may not recognize on your own. Look for common themes in what people share with you.

2. **Observe your interactions** for one week. Pay attention to when you feel most engaged and when challenges arise. Note patterns in how you communicate and how others respond.

3. **List three tasks** that energize you and three that drain you. Understanding what gives and takes your energy can help you align your work with your strengths and values.

4. **Schedule a 10-minute time block** to walk around and converse with team members. Inspired by MBWA (managing by walking around), this simple action helps build stronger relationships and encourages open communication. For remote team members, a quick but low-key, no-agenda phone call, messaging chat, or spontaneous conversation at the end of a virtual meeting can create similar connections.

3

Harness the Power of DISC:
Your Fast Track to Understanding People

Before we dive into DISC, take a moment to reflect on what you've learned so far. Understanding yourself is a journey, and the TriMetrix EQ Coaching Report provides insights that serve as a crucial foundation. If you haven't completed it yet, we strongly encourage you to do so—you'll gain the most value from this chapter by applying those personal insights to what we are about to explore.

DISC is not just a tool for managers—it is for everyone. When individuals at all levels of an organization commit to understanding themselves and others, the entire culture shifts. Teams communicate more effectively, trust deepens, and the organization as a whole becomes more cohesive. This chapter continues your journey toward self-awareness and stronger connections, reinforcing the idea that when everyone works on themselves, the entire team benefits.

WHAT IS DISC?

DISC is a powerful assessment tool that helps you understand how people behave and communicate.

It breaks down behavior into four core dimensions—*dominance, influence, steadiness,* and *compliance*—so that you can better connect with others, build stronger relationships, and lead with greater impact.

Each dimension has two primary styles based on the high and low scores in each dimension. How those styles combine to become your unique behavioral style is described in your TriMetrix EQ Coaching Report.

By developing a deeper understanding of your behavioral style, you'll see how your tendencies influence the way you interact with others, both in your professional and personal life. This is not about labels or rigid categories—it is about learning how to adapt, connect, and bring out the best in yourself and those around you.

THREE FUNDAMENTAL PRINCIPLES OF DISC

At its core, DISC helps you understand and improve how you interact with others. The process is built around three key principles:

1. UNDERSTAND YOUR OWN STYLE

The first step is self-awareness—learning how your natural tendencies shape the way you communicate, lead, and collaborate. Many people go through life without fully realizing how they come across to others.

Consider Sarah, for example. She always thought of herself as easygoing and approachable, but her high C and S scores meant she rarely spoke up in meetings. Others mistook her quiet nature for disinterest when in reality, she was simply processing information before responding. Understanding her DISC profile helped her find ways to engage more confidently.

2. RECOGNIZE THE STYLES OF OTHER PEOPLE

Just as important as knowing yourself is recognizing the behavioral tendencies of others. Some people thrive on high-energy discussions, while others prefer a methodical, step-by-step approach. When everyone in an organization builds this awareness, team dynamics improve significantly.

A manager who knows their analytical team member needs time to think before responding will avoid pressuring them for immediate answers. Similarly, an extroverted leader can recognize when they're overwhelming quieter colleagues and adjust accordingly.

3. ADAPT TO OTHERS, FOSTERING BETTER COMMUNICATION AND RELATIONSHIPS

The ultimate goal of DISC is not just understanding styles but using that knowledge to build stronger relationships. Adaptation doesn't mean changing who you are—it means making small adjustments to communicate in ways that others will receive best.

When adapting, someone with a high I score might seek to understand and ask for input rather than dominating a discussion. A person with a high S might push themselves to speak up more often in key meetings. The ability to adjust your communication style enhances team collaboration and builds stronger, more effective relationships.

D, I, S, AND C STYLES

The *dominance* dimension of DISC describes how we deal with problems and challenges. Someone with a high D score is described as a **direct** style. They tend to be decisive, goal-focused, and not afraid to take charge. They value results, thrive in challenges, and often say what others are thinking. If you want something done fast, ask someone with a high D—but don't expect them to sugarcoat things! In contrast, someone with a low D score is described as having a **reflective** style and a mild manner, preferring to work with others to achieve outcomes while avoiding conflict.

Someone with a high I (*influence* dimension) score has an **outgoing** style, and they love connecting with others. The I dimension describes how we react to people and contacts. Optimistic and enthusiastic, individuals with high I scores can be creative problem-solvers and great negotiators. On the other hand, someone with a low I score usually shows a **reserved** style and they are good at asking the hard questions and thinking about the practical details. They prefer communicating with facts and figures rather than emotions.

The S (*steadiness*) dimension is about our preferences around pace and consistency. Someone with a high S score has a **steady** style with preferences for a more measured approach to their work. Slow to warm up to others, a person with a high S style is people-oriented, considerate, and accepting of others. In contrast, someone with a low S score has a **dynamic** style and usually prefers fast-moving projects and is comfortable with conflict.

Someone with a high C (*compliance* dimension) score is likely to display a **rigorous** style, since the C dimension evaluates our reactions to procedures and constraints. A person with a high C score tends to be careful, low-key, and logical. They know how to ask great questions and focus on quality. In contrast, someone with a low C score usually has a **pioneering** style and is not concerned with established processes or procedures. They are often outspoken and independent.

While the four dimensions of DISC describe behaviors we have all observed in others, each of us is a unique combination of tendencies in each of the DISC dimensions. Any high single style is affected by high and low tendencies in the other three dimensions.

A DIRECT APPROACH CAN GET IN THE WAY: MARK

Mark had always seen himself as an efficient and decisive leader, someone who kept the team moving forward at all costs. He thought his direct style was a strength—until he reviewed the DISC section in his TriMetrix EQ report. The results opened his eyes to something he hadn't realized before: his fast-paced, results-driven communication made some of his team members hesitant to share concerns. They saw him as intimidating rather than inspiring. One section of his report even said he wants people to "be brief, then be gone."

This realization didn't hit him immediately. It wasn't until a routine team meeting that he noticed something was off. He had just proposed a change in a frequently used process and asked for feedback, but the room was unusually quiet. Looking around, he saw some hesitant faces. He turned to Michele, one of his most reliable team members. "Michele, what do you think about the change?"

She hesitated before replying. "Honestly, I had some concerns but I figured you'd already made up your mind, so I didn't bring them up."

That moment was a wake-up call. Mark realized that his approach was shutting down valuable input. He wasn't creating a space where others felt comfortable contributing. Through our Foundations program, Mark learned how to leverage the results in his personalized report to understand his natural tendencies and the impact they had on his team. This newfound awareness gave him the tools to make a conscious effort to change.

Instead of rushing to provide solutions, he started asking more open-ended questions. He made a point to truly listen, rather than just waiting for his turn to speak. He also began pausing before offering his own thoughts, allowing space for others to weigh in first.

Within a few months, the difference was noticeable. More team members spoke up, ideas flowed more freely, and decisions improved. By simply adjusting how he communicated, Mark fostered a more open and engaged team. His small changes reinforced the principle that leadership requires creating an environment where everyone feels heard and valued.

THINK ABOUT HOW OTHERS MAY SEE YOU

Just as Mark discovered, the way we perceive ourselves isn't always how others experience us. While we judge ourselves by our intentions, others only see our behaviors. This disconnect can create misunderstandings, missed opportunities, and even tension in relationships. That's why it's essential to consider how others see you.

Take Emily, for instance. She always prided herself on being a calm and focused professional. She preferred listening over speaking, making sure she processed all the information before responding. But in group meetings, her colleagues often saw her silence as disengagement. Some even assumed she wasn't interested in contributing. Through our Foundations program, Emily learned how to leverage DISC to understand how her natural tendencies were affecting team dynamics. Once she recognized this gap between how she saw herself and how others saw her, she began making subtle changes—offering brief affirmations in discussions, making eye contact more intentionally, and sharing her thoughts earlier in conversations. These small adjustments made a huge difference in how her team interacted with her. For instance, if you are more reserved and prefer to sit in the back of a room in large group activities, others may view you as unfriendly or assume you don't want to be there, even if that's not accurate.

The way people perceive us can either strengthen or hinder our relationships. While you don't need to change who you are, being mindful of how others interpret your behavior can help you build stronger connections. If you tend to be direct, do your coworkers find that refreshing, or does it come across as too aggressive? If you prefer to stay quiet in meetings, do others view that as thoughtful or disengaged? These are the questions that help bridge the gap between self-awareness and meaningful communication. You may not be aware that your behavior communicates this, but you can adapt in those circumstances—giving others a more accurate impression of you.

The key to making the most of your DISC insights is accountability. Whether you are working through this with a coach, a mentor, or on your own, taking the time to reflect and apply what you've learned is crucial. Consider discussing your results with a trusted colleague, mentor, or manager who can offer feedback on how your style influences your interactions.

If you work in a team setting, initiating conversations about communication preferences can enhance collaboration. For example, ask your coworkers how they like to receive feedback or approach problem-solving. These discussions don't require formal assessments—simply being intentional about understanding different styles can lead to stronger connections and improved team dynamics. What will you do with this information? The DISC section in your report outlines the best ways to communicate with you. Who needs to know this? Make a plan for sharing it with those people, whether that's a family member, your manager, a colleague you work closely with, or your team.

The true power of DISC lies in what you do with this knowledge. Now that you've explored your own tendencies and how they influence your relationships, what's your next step? Will you adjust how you communicate to better connect with colleagues? Will you seek feedback from those around you?

THE MOST EFFECTIVE PEOPLE ARE THOSE WHO TAKE INSIGHTS LIKE THESE AND TURN THEM INTO ACTION.

Start small, be intentional, and see how refining your communication strengthens your relationships both at work and in life.

Chapter 3 Action Items

1. **Highlight statements in the DISC section of your report** that resonate with you. Identify specific examples of how those behaviors play out in your professional and personal life.

2. **Share your DISC results** with a spouse, manager, mentor, or trusted colleague, and seek feedback on how they perceive your behavioral tendencies.

3. **Create a plan** to adapt one behavioral tendency you believe could be adjusted to better connect with others in the workplace.

4. **Practice recognizing the DISC styles** of those around you. Begin by observing their communication preferences and consider ways to adapt your approach to better engage with them.

5. **Explore the book's additional resources** at BuildingARockstarWorkforce.com to access supplementary exercises designed to help you deepen your understanding and apply your TriMetrix EQ results in real-world scenarios.

4

Unlock What Drives You:
The Key to Engagement, Fulfillment, and Impact

What drives you? Why do you make certain decisions, take specific actions, or feel more engaged in some tasks than others? Your unique set of internal motivators—your Driving Forces—shape the way you work, collaborate, and find fulfillment in what you do. Unlike skills or behaviors that you can learn and adapt, your driving forces are deeply ingrained, influencing the work that energizes you and the environments where you thrive.

Understanding what drives you is the key to unlocking your full potential. In *Building a Rockstar Workforce*, we emphasize that leadership isn't about titles—it is about understanding what truly motivates you and leveraging those strengths to create meaningful impact. When you align your work with what naturally motivates you, you perform at a higher level, feel more engaged, and experience greater satisfaction. This doesn't just benefit you—it strengthens your team, improves collaboration, and helps create a workplace where people are truly invested in what they do.

In this chapter, you'll explore what motivates you and how that can be measured using the 12 Driving Forces assessment from TTI—which includes scores for six key motivators, each with two distinct sides for a total of 12 individual driving forces—to provide insight into what fuels your decisions and priorities.

THE 12 DRIVING FORCES – A BRIEF OVERVIEW (NOT A TRAINING MANUAL)

While driving forces play a crucial role in hiring and team development, they also serve as a foundation for understanding individual motivations and workplace dynamics. To fully harness their potential, it's important to explore the six core motivators and their corresponding 12 Driving Forces. The following six motivators are each divided into two distinct sides. This deeper understanding allows you to align your work with what naturally drives you, leading to a more fulfilling career and stronger team collaboration.

- The **knowledge** motivator is about information, learning, and discovery.

  - *Instinctive* people are passionate about finding the information they need so they can leverage it.

  - *Intellectual* people love learning new information and knowledge simply for the sake of learning.

- The **utility** motivator is about practicality and return on investment for time, talent, and resources.

  - *Selfless* people want to participate for the sake of their contribution and they don't want a reward.

  - *Resourceful* people value return on investment, practical results, and they always have a reason, an end goal in mind, for their actions.

- **Surroundings** as a motivator is about beauty and form.

  - *Objective* people are interested in the functionality of their environment.

- *Harmonious* people are looking for great experiences and are interested in how their environment makes them feel.

⚈ The **others** motivator is about how you choose to help others.

- *Intentional* people choose to have strategic relationships that will provide them with a benefit, rather than offering assistance solely for the sake of giving.

- *Altruistic* people want to help others for the sake of the benefit others will gain.

⚈ The **power** motivator relates to status, control, and personal influence.

- *Collaborative* people want to make a contribution but they don't crave recognition.

- *Commanding* people want recognition, opportunities for advancement, and to be in charge.

⚈ **Methodologies** as a motivator is about the importance of structure and tradition.

- *Receptive* people are looking for new ideas and ways to improve on the existing methods, continuously looking for new possibilities.

- *Structured* people have a reason for everything they do and love to uphold traditions and proven strategies.

Whether you are driven by learning, efficiency, innovation, structure, collaboration, or making an impact, recognizing your driving forces can help you find more meaning in your work and connect with others more effectively.

BY IDENTIFYING AND LEVERAGING WHAT IS IMPORTANT TO YOU, YOU CAN CREATE A MORE FULFILLING CAREER, WORK ENVIRONMENT, AND LEADERSHIP PRESENCE—WHETHER YOU HAVE A FORMAL LEADERSHIP ROLE OR NOT.

WHY UNDERSTANDING YOUR DRIVING FORCES MATTERS

Your driving forces shape not only your work habits but also your level of satisfaction. Take, for example, Jenn, a marketing professional who always felt drained in her previous job. She loved coming up with creative campaigns but was constantly stuck in administrative tasks. When she took the 12 Driving Forces assessment, she realized she was highly *receptive*—driven by exploring new ideas and breaking away from rigid processes.

At first, Jenn wasn't sure how to make a change. She started by discussing her results with her manager, identifying small opportunities to contribute more creatively. She began taking on brainstorming sessions, pitching ideas, and collaborating on marketing strategies. Within months, her role evolved to better align with her driving forces. Not only did her enthusiasm return, but her company saw increased engagement as well.

By shifting into a role where she could experiment with innovative strategies and advocate for her strengths, Jenn found her passion reignited and her impact on the company grew.

By developing a deep awareness of your own driving forces, you not only improve your own career satisfaction but also contribute to building a rockstar workforce. When individuals understand what drives them, they bring greater energy and engagement to their roles. This creates a ripple effect throughout the organization—teams function more effectively, workplace culture improves, and the business thrives. Success depends not only on leadership at the top but also on empowering talent at every level to contribute in ways that align with their natural motivators.

THE IMPACT OF DRIVING FORCES ON WORKPLACE ENGAGEMENT AND PERFORMANCE

Have you ever worked with someone who seemed completely disengaged? Chances are that their work didn't align with what truly motivated them. When employees operate in sync with their driving forces, they feel energized and committed to their work.

Consider Alex, a project manager whose primary driver is *structured*— he thrives in environments where processes are clear and predictable. After years of success at a well-established general contractor known for its methodical approach, he accepted a promotion at a newer, more innovative construction firm that prided itself on being an early adopter of technology and flexible processes. While the move came with more responsibility and opportunity, Alex quickly found himself struggling with the company's receptive culture. The frequent shifts in project management tools, evolving methodologies, and emphasis on innovation left him feeling uncertain and overwhelmed.

At first, Alex resisted the changes, frustrated by the lack of consistency he had relied on in his previous role. But over time, he worked with his new team to find a balance. He identified areas where structured processes could improve efficiency without stifling innovation. By becoming a bridge between structured and receptive approaches, Alex not only found a way to succeed in his new environment but also helped his department streamline operations while maintaining its innovative edge.

ENGAGED EMPLOYEES DON'T JUST WORK HARDER—
THEY WORK SMARTER AND WITH GREATER ENTHUSIASM.

When companies recognize how different driving forces impact workplace adaptation, they can support employees in navigating transitions more effectively.

Recognizing and aligning driving forces is also a powerful tool in the hiring process. Organizations that incorporate driving forces assessments into their recruitment strategies can ensure new hires are set up for long-term success in roles that match their natural motivations.

HIRING WITH DRIVING FORCES: FINDING THE RIGHT FIT

Hiring the right people requires more than just assessing skills and experience. It also means aligning candidates with the motivations that will drive their success in the role. However, using driving forces in hiring isn't meant to eliminate candidates who don't perfectly match a job profile. It's about creating informed discussions that set both the employee and the company up for success. When organizations use this insight to make better hiring decisions, they reduce costly turnover, improve employee satisfaction, and build teams that are naturally aligned with their workplace culture.

What if the company Alex joined had used driving forces assessments as part of their hiring process? If they had taken the time to define the key motivators needed for success in the role, they might have identified that a receptive driver—a person who thrives in fast-moving, innovation-driven environments—was essential for long-term success in their company culture.

If Alex had taken the assessment before accepting the job, he and his new employer could have had an open conversation about his structured driver and whether it would be a good fit in an environment where processes were constantly evolving. Instead of struggling to adapt, Alex might have opted for a role in a company where structure and predictability were valued, or the company could have adjusted expectations to better support his strengths.

CREATING A JOB PROFILE WITH DRIVING FORCES

Before beginning the hiring process, organizations should define the driving forces that align best with the role. Here are some examples:

- A role requiring deep research and analysis might be best suited for someone with a strong intellectual driver.

- A sales position might benefit from a commanding driver, where the individual is motivated by achieving results and recognition.

- A customer support role could be ideal for a person with an altruistic driver, motivated by genuinely helping others.

By identifying these key motivators, hiring managers can use them as an additional data point when assessing candidates.

USING DRIVING FORCES IN THE INTERVIEW PROCESS

While driving forces should not be the sole deciding factor in hiring, they provide valuable insights into how a candidate may align with a position. During interviews, hiring managers can look for a candidate's driving forces in several ways:

- Ask questions that reveal a candidate's natural motivations.

- Present real workplace scenarios to assess how candidates respond based on their driving forces.

- Compare assessment results with job requirements to determine alignment.

This approach ensures that new hires are not only capable but also naturally inclined to thrive in their roles, leading to greater engagement and retention.

BALANCING FIT WITH FLEXIBILITY

Using driving forces in hiring doesn't mean that candidates who don't perfectly match the job profile should be excluded. It simply provides another layer of insight for making informed hiring decisions. A well-rounded team benefits from diverse motivators, and some candidates may successfully adapt to a role even if their driving forces don't align perfectly.

HOW TO LEVERAGE THE DRIVING FORCES ASSESSMENT RESULTS

Self-awareness forms the foundation for effectively leveraging driving forces. Rather than memorizing all 12 driving forces, the goal is to first understand your own unique combination of drivers and how they shape your decisions and engagement. Once you grasp your own drivers, you can start to see how they influence your daily interactions, work preferences, and career satisfaction. By building this awareness, you position yourself to make more informed decisions about your role, your contributions, and your professional growth.

Your driving forces fall into three distinct clusters, which provide insight into how your motivations influence daily work and decision-making:

- *Primary driving forces:* These are your top four drivers that strongly influence your behavior and decision-making. They provide energy, motivation, and focus. When you work in alignment with these forces, you experience high engagement and fulfillment.

- *Situational driving forces:* The middle four drivers in your profile. These factors do not significantly energize or drain you but can be activated depending on the situation or environment.

- *Indifferent driving forces:* The lowest four drivers, which have little to no impact on your daily work and motivation. These are areas where you are least interested or engaged, and tasks related to these forces may feel uninspiring or even draining.

Understanding these clusters helps you make better decisions about role alignment, career growth, and team collaboration. By prioritizing work that aligns with your primary driving forces, you can maximize your performance and satisfaction while also recognizing which tasks may require additional effort or external support.

USING DRIVING FORCES TO ALIGN WITH THE RIGHT JOB

So far, we've explored how businesses can use driving forces to hire the right people, but what about you? If you want to grow in your career or find a job that truly fulfills you, how can you use this knowledge for yourself?

Just as companies create job profiles based on the motivations best suited for a role, you can do the same when evaluating career opportunities. Instead of focusing solely on job descriptions, salaries, or company reputation, ask yourself, *Does this role align with what naturally drives me?*

Start by reflecting on your *primary driving forces*—the four motivations that influence your decisions the most. If you're highly *intellectual*, does the role offer opportunities to conduct research and expand your knowledge? If you're strongly *resourceful*, will you have the ability to maximize efficiency and drive measurable results?

During job interviews, don't just prepare to answer questions—ask your own. Find out if the work environment and leadership style align with your motivators. If collaboration fuels you, ask how teams work together. If structure is important, inquire about the company's processes. These insights can help you avoid roles that might drain your energy and instead guide you toward a job where you can thrive.

By applying driving forces to your job search and career growth, you take an active role in shaping your professional journey. The right job is about finding an environment where you are naturally motivated to succeed.

APPLYING DRIVING FORCES IN YOUR WORK AND CAREER

Once you understand what naturally energizes you, you can make intentional choices that create a more fulfilling and productive work experience. Identifying the areas where your primary driving forces are most aligned with your role helps you maximize engagement, effectiveness, and satisfaction.

One of the biggest misconceptions in professional development is the belief that leadership is reserved for those with a title. In reality, everyone has the potential to be a leader by taking ownership of their work and making intentional decisions that align with their strengths. Whether you're a frontline employee, a team contributor, or a department head, recognizing and leveraging your driving forces helps you lead yourself and influence those around you in a meaningful way. When every team member steps into their strengths, organizations become more agile, collaborative, and successful.

UNDERSTANDING THE DRIVING FORCES OF OTHERS

Once you have clarity on your own driving forces, you can begin to recognize and appreciate the motivations of those around you. This awareness strengthens collaboration, reduces friction, and fosters an environment where people can contribute at their best. Just like behavioral styles, understanding what motivates your colleagues helps you communicate more effectively, delegate tasks that align with their strengths, and foster a culture of appreciation and respect.

For example, if a team member has a high *intellectual* driver, they may feel most engaged when their role involves continuous learning, conducting in-depth research, and exploring new ideas to solve complex problems. Someone with a strong *collaborative* driver will thrive in team-oriented projects and shared decision-making environments. By leveraging these insights, teams can create an environment where each person's contributions are maximized.

USING DRIVING FORCES FOR PROFESSIONAL GROWTH

Your driving forces can also serve as a guide for professional development. When choosing training programs, mentorship opportunities, or career advancement paths, prioritize those that align with your motivations. If you are *receptive*, seek opportunities where creative thinking and innovation are rewarded. If you are *commanding*, look for leadership roles where you can take ownership of key initiatives.

Whether you're evaluating career opportunities, navigating team dynamics, or seeking professional growth, using your driving forces as a guide allows you to make more intentional choices that lead to long-term success. The more aligned your work is with your core motivators, the greater your contribution will be—not just for yourself, but for those around you as well.

Chapter 4 Action Items

1. **Identify your primary driving forces** by reviewing your assessment results and reflecting on how they show up in your work and daily life.

2. **Compare your job responsibilities** to your driving forces to see if your work aligns with what naturally energizes you. If not, consider small adjustments.

3. **Have a conversation** with your manager or mentor about how your driving forces influence your work and explore ways to align your role more effectively.

4. **Make small shifts** in your daily tasks to better align with your driving forces, such as taking on innovative projects if you are *receptive* or seeking input from others if you are *collaborative*.

5. **Reflect on areas where your work conflicts** with your driving forces and create a plan to adjust your role or environment to support your natural motivators.

5

Strengthen the Leadership Muscles That Matter

What if the key to your career growth wasn't about working harder, but about working smarter? Competencies—the skills and abilities that help you excel—play a crucial role in building a rockstar workforce. No matter your role, developing the right competencies will set you apart and position you for success. This chapter is about identifying the competencies that matter most to you and crafting a plan to sharpen them.

UNDERSTANDING COMPETENCIES

Competencies are more than just skills—they're the building blocks of personal and professional growth. They help you navigate challenges, lead projects, and create meaningful impact in your work. Whether you're an entry-level employee or an experienced executive, developing the right competencies can elevate your contributions and create new opportunities.

TAKE A MOMENT TO REFLECT

What skills have helped you succeed so far? Where do you struggle? This chapter will guide you through identifying your strengths and areas for growth.

TECHNICAL SKILLS VERSUS COMPETENCIES: WHY YOU NEED BOTH

It's important to understand that competencies do not replace technical skills—both are essential for professional success. Technical skills are the specialized abilities required to perform specific job functions, such as coding, financial analysis, operating machinery, or designing marketing campaigns. These skills are industry- and job-specific, and they often require formal education or training.

Competencies, on the other hand, are the transferable skills that allow people to apply their technical expertise effectively. Competencies such as decision-making, time and priority management, interpersonal skills, and problem-solving determine how well you execute your technical skills, collaborate with others, and navigate workplace challenges.

For example, an IT professional may need technical knowledge in programming languages, but without strong problem-solving and time management skills, they may struggle to debug software efficiently or meet project deadlines. Likewise, a nurse requires medical training, but interpersonal skills and resiliency are just as crucial when dealing with patients and high-pressure situations.

> TO BUILD A ROCKSTAR WORKFORCE, YOU MUST DEVELOP BOTH YOUR TECHNICAL EXPERTISE AND THE COMPETENCIES THAT ALLOW YOU TO APPLY THOSE SKILLS EFFECTIVELY IN DYNAMIC ENVIRONMENTS.

If you focus solely on technical ability but neglect competencies, you may find it challenging to adapt, lead, or grow in your career.

THE 25 CORE COMPETENCIES

Here is a list of 25 competencies that are crucial for professional success:

- Diplomacy – Effectively and tactfully handling difficult or sensitive issues.

- Interpersonal skills – Effectively communicating, building rapport, and relating well to all kinds of people.

- Leadership – Organizing and influencing people to believe in a vision while creating a sense of purpose and direction.

- Employee development/coaching – Facilitating, supporting, and contributing to the professional growth of others.

- Self-starting – Demonstrating initiative and willingness to begin working.

- Goal orientation – Setting, pursuing, and attaining goals, regardless of obstacles or circumstances.

- Understanding others – Understanding the uniqueness and contributions of others.

- Resiliency – Quickly recovering from adversity.

- Decision-making – Analyzing all aspects of a situation to make consistently sound and timely decisions.

- Flexibility – Readily modifying, responding, and adapting to change with minimal resistance.

- Creativity and innovation – Creating new approaches, designs, processes, technologies, and/or systems to achieve the desired result.

- Influencing others – Personally affecting others' actions, decisions, opinions, or thinking.

- Futuristic thinking – Imagining, envisioning, projecting, and/or creating what has not yet been actualized.

- Planning and organizing – Establishing courses of action to ensure that work is completed effectively.

- Problem-solving – Defining, analyzing, and diagnosing key components of a problem to formulate a solution.

- Project management – Identifying and overseeing resources, tasks, systems, and people to obtain results.

- Negotiation – Listening to many points of view and facilitating agreements between two or more parties.

- Conceptual thinking – Analyzing hypothetical situations, patterns, and/or abstract concepts to formulate connections and new insights.

- Teamwork – Cooperating with others to meet objectives.

- Continuous learning – Taking initiative to regularly learn new concepts, technologies, and/or methods.

- Personal accountability – Being answerable for personal actions.

- Time and priority management – Prioritizing and completing tasks in order to deliver desired outcomes within allotted time frames.

- Conflict management – Understanding, addressing, and resolving conflict constructively.

- Customer focus – Anticipating, meeting, and/or exceeding customer needs, wants, and expectations.

- Appreciating others – Identifying with and caring about others.

Which of these resonate with you? Highlight the ones you believe are most important for your role and future growth. Don't worry about mastering all 25—focus on three to five that will make the biggest difference in your role right now. Then, continue to reflect on this list as you make progress and select additional competencies to focus on as needed.

ESSENTIAL COMPETENCIES FOR EVERYONE

While all 25 competencies are important, some are foundational to success in any role. Based on our experience working with people across industries at all levels, we believe these five core competencies are essential for everyone to develop:

- Time and priority management

- Interpersonal skills

- Personal accountability

- Decision-making

- Continuous learning

If you're unsure where to begin, we recommend focusing on these competencies first. They will provide a strong foundation for growth and success in any career.

HOW TO CHOOSE THE RIGHT COMPETENCIES FOR YOU

Selecting the right competencies starts with self-reflection and strategy. Use these steps to guide your decision:

1. **Self-assessment**: Think about your daily responsibilities. What skills do you rely on? Which ones could you improve?

2. **Peer feedback**: Ask colleagues or mentors for their perspective. What do they see as your strengths? Where could you grow?

3. **Career aspirations**: Consider where you want to be in three to five years. What competencies will help you get there?

4. **Job requirements**: Look at job descriptions for roles you aspire to. What skills do they emphasize?

Once you've identified three to five core competencies, commit to strengthening them.

DEVELOPING YOUR COMPETENCIES

Here's how you can actively develop your chosen competencies:

- **Practice daily**: Look for opportunities in your current role to use and refine these skills.

- **Learn from others**: Find a mentor or observe colleagues who excel in these areas.

- **Seek training**: Take courses, read books, or attend workshops.

- **Get feedback**: Regularly ask for input from peers and supervisors on your progress.

- **Track your growth**: Keep a journal of your improvements and challenges to stay accountable.

- **Explore the book's additional resources** at BuildingARockstarWorkforce.com to access supplementary exercises designed to help develop your chosen competencies.

To illustrate how developing competencies can create real change, let's look at Josh's story. Josh, a mid-level supervisor at a Phoenix-based software company, was constantly overwhelmed. His days were packed with meetings, urgent emails, and last-minute fires to put out. Despite frequently working late, he often felt like he wasn't making real progress. He struggled to prioritize effectively, and the constant stress was leading to burnout.

When he joined the Rockstar Workforce four-month Foundations program, he committed to working on the *time and priority management* competency in the first month. With the support of his cohort and facilitator, he developed a plan:

Month 1: Josh identified his biggest time drains and implemented a structured to-do list with clear priorities each morning.

Month 2: He started using time-blocking techniques to protect focus time and reduce distractions.

Month 3: Josh worked on delegating more effectively, recognizing that he had been holding onto tasks that his team could handle.

Month 4: His group continued checking in on his progress, reinforcing his accountability and solidifying new habits.

By the end of the program, Josh had transformed his workflow. He was leaving the office on time, completing high-impact projects efficiently, and leading his team with greater confidence. Instead of feeling like he was constantly behind, he was in control of his schedule. The structured accountability from the program had made all the difference.

COMMON PITFALLS TO AVOID

As you embark on developing your competencies, be mindful of common mistakes that can hinder progress:

- **Trying to improve too many competencies at once**: Focus on three to five key areas instead of spreading yourself too thin.

- **Not tracking progress**: Keep a journal or set measurable milestones to monitor improvement.

- **Avoiding feedback**: Seeking input from peers and mentors can help refine your approach.

- **Skipping accountability**: Without check-ins or accountability partners, progress can stall.

By recognizing and avoiding these pitfalls, you can stay on track and maximize your growth.

BUILDING A ROCKSTAR WORKFORCE THROUGH COMPETENCIES

A rockstar workforce isn't built on titles—it's built on talent. When everyone in an organization commits to sharpening their skills, the entire team thrives. This is accomplished by creating an environment where each person brings their best to the table.

Imagine if every member of your team mastered just one additional competency. How much stronger would your organization be? Developing competencies is a game-changer for company culture and success.

REFLECTION EXERCISE: IDENTIFYING YOUR COMPETENCIES

Take a few minutes to reflect on your career and daily responsibilities:

- When was the last time you felt truly effective in your role? What competencies contributed to that success?

- Which competency, if improved, would have the biggest impact on your work?

- What challenges do you face daily that could be addressed by refining specific skills?

- How would strengthening these competencies influence your long-term career trajectory?

Write your answers down and use them to guide your competency development plan.

Chapter 5 Action Items

1. **Identify your core competencies** by reviewing the list of 25 competencies and choosing three to five that are most important for your current role or future career aspirations.

2. **Create a competency development plan** by outlining one specific action you will take to improve each of your selected competencies over the next month.

3. **Track your progress** weekly by keeping a journal or digital log to note your efforts, challenges, and improvements in your chosen competencies.

4. **Schedule a self-check-in** by setting a reminder for 30 or 60 days from now to evaluate whether you have improved in your chosen competencies, and adjust your plan as needed.

6

Dynamic Communication:
Adapt Your Words, Expand Your Influence

Communication is one of the most essential skills for both professional and personal success because it forms the foundation of every relationship. Whether you're collaborating with a team, guiding a project, or simply having a conversation, communication is how we connect, understand, and influence others.

However, when communication breaks down, the results can be costly—missed opportunities, confusion, frustration, and damaged trust. Imagine a scenario where a critical client request needs urgent attention, but the message isn't clearly communicated. One person assumes it's low priority, another thinks someone else is handling it, and a third isn't even aware of it. By the time the deadline arrives, nothing is done. The outcome? Disappointed clients, finger-pointing, and wasted effort.

This type of breakdown happens all too often, but it's avoidable with dynamic communication. More than just speaking, dynamic communication is about listening, adapting, and verifying mutual understanding. When individuals at every level refine this skill, they collaborate more effectively, reduce misunderstandings, and create stronger, more productive relationships.

Dynamic communication is about achieving results through collaboration, ensuring that individuals can work together—sometimes a difficult task, but crucial to a successful outcome. However, even with the best intentions, communication can still break down. Misunderstandings, unclear expectations, and differing communication styles can lead to frustration and conflict. Recognizing these challenges allows us to proactively adapt our communication strategies and prevent potential conflicts before they escalate.

CONFLICT MANAGEMENT REQUIRES EFFECTIVE COMMUNICATION

Navigating conflict is a crucial part of effective communication, which will be explored further in chapter 12. Since managing conflict is fundamentally about communication, developing communication skills ensures that everyone can collaborate productively and maintain positive workplace relationships. Without a strong grasp of communication skills, you are at a disadvantage when conflict arises.

In our training, we take the communication skill concept one step further by calling it dynamic because effective communication is all about adapting your style and your message to reach others. Dynamic communication is an approach focused on adapting to different types of people and communication styles. It's essential to build those connections to create the trust you must have to successfully navigate conflict and change.

Effective communication is not just about getting your point across—it's also about preventing misunderstandings before they occur. Dynamic communication plays a key role in setting the right tone from the start, whether you're meeting someone for the first time, responding to a stressful situation, or delivering an important message.

BY LEARNING TO RECOGNIZE HOW OTHERS PERCEIVE YOUR WORDS, TONE, AND BODY LANGUAGE, YOU CAN CREATE A STRONGER CONNECTION AND REDUCE THE RISK OF MISCOMMUNICATION.

The ability to "read" the room or a person's mood is essential to create a moment of connection with them as well as help you know how to adapt to get your message across effectively.

BETTER COMMUNICATION IS A LEARNED SKILL

Some people are naturally wired and are good at making connections, while others have to practice. Take, for example, someone who struggles with small talk and networking. They might find social interactions exhausting or anxiety-inducing, leading them to avoid conversations altogether.

However, by consciously practicing active listening, asking open-ended questions, and paying attention to body language, they can gradually improve their ability to connect with others and feel more confident in social situations.

Over time, what once felt unnatural becomes more comfortable, showing that communication is a skill that can be developed with effort and intentional practice.

This includes having more conversations, actively listening, and seeking feedback. By taking small, deliberate steps—such as preparing discussion points before meetings or practicing nonverbal communication skills—individuals can develop stronger communication habits over time. For example, someone who struggles with engaging in meetings might start by preparing a few thoughtful questions or comments in advance, gradually building their confidence and communication skills over time. This skill is about reading both the situation and the person, then adapting to them.

In my role, I (Adam) frequently find myself in front of new groups, leading them through various development programs. It's common for me to facilitate sessions for three or four different groups, with different companies, in a single week. I'm constantly working to establish rapport and connect with people quickly. Given my career, many assume I'm an extrovert, but the reality is different. On the DISC graph, my I score (influence) hovers right around the middle, meaning that while I can be engaging, it takes conscious effort and energy to adapt to new environments and connect with different personalities. To make this process more effective, I've learned to be intentional—focusing on reading the room, adjusting my communication style, and making meaningful connections. This doesn't come naturally to everyone, but it's a skill that can be developed with practice and awareness.

DYNAMIC MEANS ADAPTATION

Put another way, dynamic communication goes beyond delivering a message by focusing on building genuine connections that encourage understanding and collaboration. The way we convey our thoughts can either build trust or create barriers. By adjusting our approach, we ensure that our message resonates, strengthens relationships, and leads to meaningful interactions. It's about being intentional, adaptive, and clear in every exchange.

Understanding how to best deliver your message means being mindful of several factors. Adjusting your tone can help ensure clarity and prevent misunderstandings, while choosing the right format—whether it's an in-person conversation, an email, or a text—can make a significant difference in how your message is received.

Additionally, considering the timing of your communication is crucial; delivering a message at the right moment enhances its impact and effectiveness. Ensuring that your message is received as intended requires careful attention to context and clarity.

For example, imagine a manager sends an email to their team saying, "We need to discuss project delays." Some team members might interpret this as an urgent problem requiring immediate attention, while others assume it's a routine check-in. Without additional context, the message can create unnecessary stress or disengagement. Clarifying intent—such as specifying the meeting's purpose and expectations—ensures the message is received as intended, preventing miscommunication and confusion.

UNDERSTANDING BEHAVIORAL STYLES IS FUNDAMENTAL TO ADAPTATION

As discussed in chapter 3, understanding DISC behavioral styles is fundamental to effective communication. Rather than revisiting the full breakdown of DISC principles, this section focuses on how to actively apply these insights in daily interactions. If you need a refresher on the core DISC styles and how they shape communication tendencies, refer back to chapter 3. You can also refer to the DISC section of your TriMetrix EQ Coaching Report for more personalized insight. Here, we'll explore practical ways to leverage that knowledge in real-world scenarios, helping you connect with others more effectively and adjust your approach dynamically. To build on DISC insights rather than repeat them, we focus on three practical ways to apply DISC principles in everyday interactions:

1. Understanding your style and how it's perceived by others:

   ❡ Recognizing how others see and interpret your communication

- Adjusting your body language, tone, and volume for clarity

- Being mindful of how your words and actions impact different audiences

2. Understanding others' communication styles:

- Identifying behavioral cues that indicate someone's preferred communication style

- Observing how people respond to direct versus indirect communication

- Recognizing when to adapt your message to fit different personalities

3. Effectively communicating across styles (adapting):

- Tailoring your communication approach to different DISC styles

- Flexing between task- and relationship-focused interactions

- Adjusting how you deliver information based on the needs of your audience

Now that we've explored how to apply DISC principles in daily interactions, remember it's important to recognize that communication is not a one-size-fits-all approach.

EACH PERSON BRINGS A UNIQUE COMBINATION OF TRAITS AND PREFERENCES THAT INFLUENCE HOW THEY COMMUNICATE AND RESPOND TO OTHERS.

Understanding these nuances allows us to refine our approach and build stronger, more meaningful connections.

We often challenge individuals to consider that they may not fully understand how others perceive them. Taking a deeper, more detailed look at your personal style and the way you come across to others can be incredibly insightful. By keeping others' behavioral styles in mind, you can begin to see beyond surface-level reactions and gain a clearer understanding of the connections you make.

To understand how someone else perceives you, first you must get a feel for what their behavioral style is, and especially how different their style is from yours. Some styles work in harmony with others, while others may clash—feeling annoying or off-putting without meaning to.

WHAT'S YOUR STYLE?

Every workplace consists of diverse communication styles, and understanding these differences is key to fostering a successful environment. Being aware of how you communicate and how others prefer to interact can significantly enhance teamwork and collaboration. Recognizing these nuances allows for more effective communication, leading to increased efficiency, reduced misunderstandings, and improved work relationships.

Here's an example:

> *Imagine working on a team where one person prefers precise and detailed communication (high C), while another prefers a more thoughtful, consensus-driven approach (high S). Without understanding these preferences, frustration can arise—one person may feel overwhelmed with detail while the other gets impatient. However, when both individuals adapt their styles, they can work more effectively together. The high C communicator can take it easy on the details and acknowledge the*

need for connection, while the high S can be more precise and structured when presenting ideas. By meeting in the middle, they create a more balanced, productive dialogue that fosters mutual respect and collaboration.

HOW TO IDENTIFY BEHAVIORAL STYLES THROUGH OBSERVATION

Think about the last time you were in a social setting with people you didn't know. For me (Adam), this happened recently at a neighbor's house during their son's birthday party. Our neighbors had invited family members we had never met, and I found myself in a situation where I needed to connect with unfamiliar people.

When meeting new people, I start by observing their behavior and energy in the environment. Some individuals make it easy by engaging in conversations, asking questions, and showing an openness to interact. Others are more reserved, naturally gravitating toward quieter spaces away from the main group. I take a moment to assess their comfort level and determine what approach will make them feel at ease.

At this party, I noticed an elderly lady, possibly one of the grandparents, standing alone and not really engaging with others. I found myself near her and didn't want to have an awkward silence. Instead of immediately introducing myself and sparking up a conversation, I eased into the dialogue by commenting on something happening in the moment, such as how much fun the kids were having.

A simple, situational observation such as this helps create an initial connection without overwhelming the other person. For me, this practice has become second nature, but for many, this level of social awareness requires conscious effort and development over time. It's a learned skill.

If this doesn't come naturally to you, don't worry. Communication is something you can work on and improve over time. This book and the TriMetrix EQ Coaching Report are great resources to help you develop these lifelong communication skills. With practice and awareness, you can enhance your ability to connect with others and become a more dynamic communicator.

COMMUNICATION STYLES CAN HAVE POSITIVE OR NEGATIVE IMPACTS

Understanding communication styles goes beyond just knowing your own tendencies; it involves recognizing and adapting to others' preferences. When communication is misaligned, collaboration suffers. But when employees learn to adjust their approaches, workplace relationships thrive.

Consider this example:

Two colleagues, one with a high I score and one with a low I score, are collaborating on a project. The high I individual thrives on social interaction, brainstorming, and thinking out loud, often generating ideas in the moment and discussing multiple possibilities before making decisions. The low I colleague, on the other hand, prefers a more structured and reserved approach, taking time to process information internally before responding.

Early in their collaboration, the high I colleague enthusiastically shared multiple ideas in quick succession, expecting an immediate exchange of energy and thoughts. The low I colleague, however, took longer to reflect and formulate responses, leading the high I to assume they were uninterested or disengaged. Meanwhile, the low I found the rapid flow of ideas overwhelming and struggled to interject their own thoughts into the conversation.

Once they recognized their differences, they adjusted their approach. The high I learned to slow down and allow space for thoughtful responses, while the low I made an effort to verbalize their thoughts more frequently to maintain engagement. By understanding and respecting each other's communication preferences, they improved collaboration and built a stronger working relationship.

This example highlights how differences in communication styles can lead to misunderstandings, but with awareness and small adjustments, collaboration becomes much more effective. The way we communicate isn't just about what we say—it's also about how we say it. Beyond words, factors like tone, body language, and timing play a crucial role in how messages are received and interpreted. Understanding these nonverbal elements can help you refine your communication even further and prevent unnecessary conflict.

THE IMPACT OF NONVERBAL COMMUNICATION ON YOUR MESSAGE

Nonverbal cues play a crucial role in workplace interactions. Research suggests that only 7% of communication is based on words, while 93% is nonverbal (tone, body language, facial expressions).

Let's review a few examples:

- **A supervisor giving feedback**: If the supervisor delivers constructive criticism with crossed arms and a furrowed brow, the message may be perceived as negative—even if the words are encouraging.

- **A team presentation**: Picture a team member presenting an idea in a meeting. They speak confidently, but their lack of eye contact and closed-off posture make them seem uncertain or unapproachable. Even though their words are strong, their body language sends a conflicting message, making it harder for others to engage with their ideas.

- **An executive announcing an organizational change**: A company executive shares a major change in direction with employees. Though the words are positive, their monotone delivery, lack of eye contact, and closed-off stance make it clear they are not excited about the change. As a result, employees feel uneasy and skeptical rather than motivated and confident.

- **A customer service interaction**: A retail employee greets a customer and asks if they need help, but their arms are crossed, their tone is flat, and they avoid eye contact. Even though the words are welcoming, the customer perceives disinterest or even annoyance, leading to a negative experience and possibly a lost sale.

Ways to improve workplace communication include these approaches:

- **Matching tone to intent**: Ensuring that enthusiasm, empathy, or authority is appropriately conveyed.

- **Observing body language**: Being mindful of posture, hand gestures, and facial expressions.

- **Adjusting intensity**: Recognizing when to be more assertive or when to soften communication for clarity.

Nonverbal communication is a powerful force that can either enhance or undermine the message you're trying to convey. Whether it's a casual conversation, a high-stakes presentation, or a performance review, being mindful of how you communicate beyond words can strengthen relationships and prevent unnecessary misunderstandings.

APPLYING NONVERBAL ADAPTATION TO YOUR COMMUNICATION

Now that we've explored the impact of body language, tone, and delivery, let's take it a step further by understanding how different communication styles interact—and how we can adapt to create more meaningful and productive exchanges.

People with more forthright, outgoing styles may not realize that their body language can communicate too aggressively for some individuals. People who are reserved, quiet, and thoughtful may be repelled or intimidated by certain aspects of communication.

The pie chart below is a classic representation of the importance of how you deliver your message. The words you use are the least effective part of the total communication received from in-person interactions.

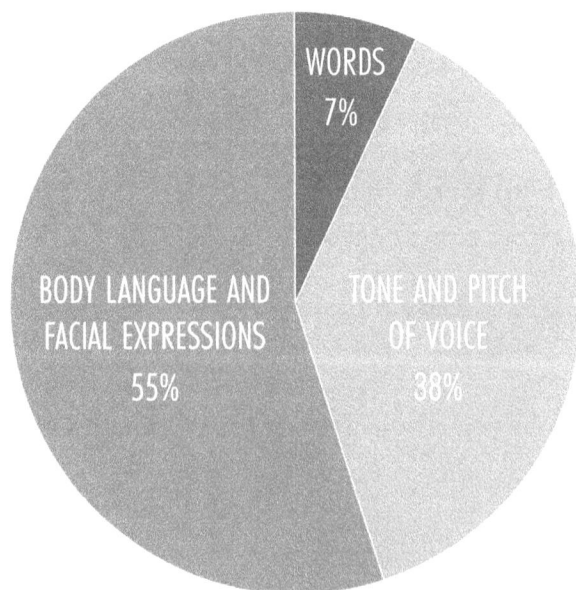

WORDS
7%

BODY LANGUAGE AND
FACIAL EXPRESSIONS
55%

TONE AND PITCH
OF VOICE
38%

Only 7% of what is being said is actually being consumed, while 55% of the communication is coming from your body language and expressions, and 38% is coming from the volume and tone of voice.[1]

This is a great reminder that just because you said something doesn't mean it was heard. This information also has real importance when you consider how much communication happens through email, text messages, phone, and virtual meetings. You don't send or receive the whole message with these mediums. For example, the impact of eye contact is essentially lost in virtual meetings because even if everyone is looking directly at their webcams, it doesn't feel the same.

Keeping this information top of mind, let's look at ways to balance behavior in face-to-face interaction:

- Eye contact:
  - Some people love eye contact and expect it, and some find it intimidating.
  - Some people will interpret a complete lack of eye contact as distrustful or weak.

- Facial expressions:
  - Smiling or not smiling when it's expected can alter the meaning of words dramatically.
  - Raising or lowering eyebrows changes meaning significantly.
  - A complete lack of facial expression can express disinterest, fear, or even dishonesty.

- Volume and tone of voice:
  - Either speaking too loudly or speaking in a flat, unvaried tone can create negative impacts.

1. Mehrabian, Albert. *Silent Messages* (Wadsworth Publishing Company, 1972).

- Speaking speed, fast or slow:

  - Nonstop talking can communicate no interest in other points of view or a desire to control the interaction.

  - Speaking too slowly or with long pauses can indicate a lack of confidence, focus, or preparedness.

- The framework of the conversation:

  - Getting sidetracked and wandering to another topic can be annoying to some.

  - Ignoring questions or comments from others can indicate a desire to dominate the conversation or simply overrun other points of view.

- Assertiveness in the message—pushing one approach without allowing other options:

  - Asking questions to determine if others are on board can soften this approach when it happens, inviting others to speak.

  - Explaining how you've considered different angles can mitigate this impression.

- Level of intensity in the conversation—this one is harder to describe, but has to do with how important the topic is and how urgent it might be to address it:

  - Not showing enough intensity can have just as much of a negative impact as being too intense.

Many of the above aspects of an interaction can be tuned to balance a too-aggressive or too-tentative style. Simply considering how you tend to communicate can help you be aware of the ways you are connecting or failing to connect.

Complicating communication even more is the fact that different behavioral styles will assign different levels of importance to your verbal and nonverbal messaging. Using DISC styles, a person with a high C style might pay more attention to the words used and less to the volume and tone, while a person with high I or high S tendencies will gravitate toward the emotional aspects of the conversation, focusing on how you're saying things and whether or not you touch the individual—yes, physically touch them!

You can use the DISC styles to think about how compatible your style is with someone else's, which is especially helpful when you're learning about your own. Some combinations of the behavioral styles are compatible and harmonious, and others are likely to take more effort to meet on common ground.

To learn more about the compatibility between different styles, visit the additional resources for this book at BuildingARockstarWorkforce.com. The charts available on the website show how the styles tend to work together, along with some pointers for how to approach different styles in good ways and poor ways, so you understand what they will and won't like. It's also helpful in most workplace and social situations to have a more instinctive set of guidelines for adapting to other behavioral styles, and the style compatibility chart also describes ways to recognize different styles and how to adapt to connect with them.

DYNAMIC COMMUNICATION IS NOT JUST ABOUT WHAT WE SAY, BUT HOW WE SAY IT—AND MORE IMPORTANTLY, HOW IT'S RECEIVED.

Throughout this chapter, we've explored how adapting communication styles, reading nonverbal cues, and understanding different behavioral tendencies can strengthen relationships and improve collaboration. By applying these insights, you can create stronger connections, prevent misunderstandings, and build trust in both professional and personal settings. As we move forward, we'll dive deeper into how these communication skills play a crucial role in managing conflict—transforming potential friction into opportunities for growth and stronger teamwork.

Chapter 6 Action Items

1. **Identify your primary communication style** based on the DISC assessment.

2. **Reflect on how your communication style might be perceived** by others.

3. **Observe and identify the communication styles** of coworkers and clients.

4. **Practice adapting your style** in different interactions this week.

7

Connecting With Others:
Building Bridges, Not Walls

Effective connections are built on strong relationships. Whether you are managing people or working as part of a team, building strong connections benefits everyone. Connecting with others is not just about communication but about fostering trust, building meaningful relationships, and understanding people at a deeper level. Success is more than achieving results—it's achieving results through collaboration. If you're managing people, fostering strong relationships enhances teamwork and trust. If you're working within a team, strengthening your connections can improve communication and overall effectiveness. Establishing genuine connections will make others feel valued, heard, and supported.

HOW DO YOU BUILD RELATIONSHIPS?

Building strong relationships requires intentional effort. The most effective leaders take the time to invest in their relationships—not just when there's work to be done, but regularly, in an authentic way. Strong relationships are built on a foundation of consistent and meaningful interactions. Here's how:

1. **Genuine interest**: People can tell when you're being authentic. Leaders who take a sincere interest in their team members' well-being build stronger, lasting relationships.

2. **Consistent engagement**: Regular check-ins, meaningful conversations, and ongoing feedback create a culture of connection.

3. **Trust and vulnerability**: Being open, honest, and showing vulnerability in the right moments encourages others to do the same.

4. **Actively listening**: It's not enough to hear the words someone says; true understanding comes from listening, asking questions, and responding in a way that makes them feel valued.

THE POWER OF SMALL INTERACTIONS

Applying these principles in real-world situations can have a profound impact on relationships, whether at work or in your personal life. Let's look at an example of how a small but intentional effort to connect can strengthen trust and engagement within a team.

Alice, a project manager, noticed that Jake, a normally engaged team member, had started to withdraw. He participated less in meetings, seemed distracted, and gave brief responses. Instead of assuming he was uninterested, Alice decided to check in during a casual coffee break.

"Hey Jake, I've noticed you've been quieter than usual. Everything okay?" she asked.

Jake hesitated before admitting he was feeling overwhelmed with his workload. Sensing an opportunity to help, Alice suggested they chat over lunch. As they talked, she actively listened and encouraged him to pinpoint what was stressing him most. Rather than simply redistributing tasks, she helped him prioritize responsibilities and suggested structured check-ins to ensure he felt supported.

Over the next few weeks, Alice followed up regularly—not just in formal meetings but through quick messages and casual check-ins. Gradually, Jake became more engaged, and his confidence returned.

What could have spiraled into burnout became an opportunity to build trust, reinforcing Alice's belief that meaningful connections aren't built through grand gestures, but through small, intentional efforts.

MEANINGFUL CONNECTIONS ARE BUILT THROUGH EVERYDAY MOMENTS OF TRUST AND ENGAGEMENT.

By taking a few minutes to check in, show support, and actively listen, you can foster relationships that lead to stronger collaboration and a more engaged team. These small interactions add up, shaping the culture of your workplace and the quality of your connections with those around you.

Small, everyday moments are the building blocks of strong relationships. Taking five minutes to check in on someone's day, remembering personal details about their lives, or simply acknowledging their hard work can make a significant impact.

A key strategy for building these connections is called managing by walking around (MBWA)—intentionally leaving your office or workstation to engage with employees, ask about their day, and observe how things are going. This simple practice builds rapport, opens communication, and shows that you truly care about your people—not just their work, but their personal well-being.

A RELATIONSHIP IS A TWO-WAY STREET

A strong relationship is not just about what you need from others but also about what you give. People who only reach out when they need something miss the opportunity to build real connections.

A meaningful relationship is built on voluntary interaction—connecting with someone not because you need something, but simply because you value the relationship. It's about checking in, showing genuine consideration, and truly caring about how they're doing, with a sincere desire to know and support them.

When you have a meaningful relationship, the interactions are consistent and operate in both directions. It can't just be when you need something. If you only reach out when you need a favor, people will see through it. You might say, "Hey, how are you? Oh, by the way, I need this done." They know you don't really care—you're just being polite before making a request. That's not building a connection; that's simply checking a box. It's a one-way street that may erode trust.

These no-strings-attached actions build genuine relationships:

- Check in with people without an agenda. Ask how they're doing and really listen to the response.

- Express appreciation and recognize efforts. A simple "I appreciate the work you put into that project" goes a long way.

- Offer support even when it's not expected. Show up for others before they ask for help.

We work with teams of all sizes, and for smaller teams, we encourage a simple rule: You must know a little bit about each person you work with. You can't just walk past someone without acknowledging them—unless you're in a genuine rush. Be intentional. Create an ongoing dialogue, letting people know you want to learn more about them both personally and professionally.

This approach isn't just for work. Think about your closest friendships. Are you putting in enough effort to maintain those relationships? Do the people you care about know how important they are to you? Are you reaching out to them regularly?

By fostering a culture of mutual respect and support, you create an environment where people feel valued, engaged, and motivated to contribute to shared success.

TAILORING YOUR COMMUNICATION FOR STRONGER CONNECTIONS

Remember when we discussed DISC behavioral styles and dynamic communication? Those concepts aren't just theories—they are real tools you can use every day to strengthen your relationships. Think back to a time when a conversation felt effortless versus a time when it felt frustrating. Chances are that the difference was how well you adapted to the other person's communication style. Whether someone thrives on data, values collaboration, or prefers concise messages, adjusting your approach can make a lasting impact. If you want to build trust and connection, start by speaking the language others understand best.

WHY SOME CONNECTIONS FAIL AND OTHERS THRIVE

Have you ever had a conversation where everything clicked—the energy was right, the discussion flowed naturally, and you left feeling understood? Now, think of a time when the opposite happened—where the connection fell flat, emotions ran high, or misunderstandings ruined the moment.

What made the difference? It might be emotional intelligence (EQ). EQ isn't just about being nice or reading the room—it's knowing when to speak and when to listen, when to challenge and when to support. The best communicators don't just say the right things; they sense what's needed in the moment and adjust their approach. EQ isn't a skill you're born with—it's something you develop. And in the next chapter, we'll show you exactly how to do it. If you're ready to transform the way you connect with others, keep reading.

Chapter 7 Action Items

1. **Identify one relationship** (personal or professional) that you want to improve. Take one small action this week to strengthen it.

2. **Use MBWA** (managing by walking around) at least once this week—engage with someone on your team in a casual, non-work-related way.

3. **Practice adapting your communication style** to someone whose DISC profile differs from yours.

4. **Check in with at least one person** this week without an agenda—no requests, just genuine interest.

8

The Advantage of Emotional Intelligence:
A Skill You Can't Ignore

You know a top-performing employee when you see one. They're the ones people gravitate toward, the ones who make collaboration seamless, the ones who can handle stress without spiraling. But what exactly makes them stand out? It's not just technical expertise or intelligence—it's their ability to manage emotions, read situations, and build relationships. In other words, it's their emotional intelligence, or EQ.

THE MISSING PIECE OF A HIGH-PERFORMING WORKFORCE

Emotional intelligence isn't just a "nice-to-have" skill for leaders. It's the foundation for effective communication, strong teamwork, and career success at every level of an organization. Whether you're leading a company, managing a team, or simply trying to improve your professional relationships, EQ is the force multiplier that determines how well you navigate workplace dynamics.

WHY SHOULD YOU CARE ABOUT EQ?

Think about the most frustrating interactions you've had at work—a manager who micromanages; a coworker who overreacts to feedback; a customer who turns a minor inconvenience into a major issue.

What do these scenarios have in common? Low emotional intelligence.

Now think about the opposite:

- A leader who remains calm and solution-oriented under pressure

- A teammate who listens, understands, and communicates effectively

- A customer service rep who can de-escalate a tense situation with ease

The difference? High emotional intelligence.

EQ affects nearly every aspect of workplace success:

- **Performance**: Studies show that 90% of top performers possess high emotional intelligence.[2]

- **Leadership**: The best leaders aren't just technically skilled; they know how to motivate and inspire others.

- **Career growth**: Promotions often go to those who handle challenges and people effectively, not just those who do great work.

- **Workplace culture**: High-EQ environments foster trust, collaboration, and engagement.

If you want to build a high-impact workforce, EQ isn't optional—it's essential. And the good news? Unlike IQ, EQ can be developed.

THE FIVE KEY SKILLS OF EQ

Before diving into strategies for developing your EQ, let's break it down. Emotional intelligence isn't about being "soft" or overly emotional. It's about developing five key skills:

1. **Self-awareness** – Recognizing your emotions and how they impact your thoughts, decisions, and behaviors.

---

2. Bradberry, Travis. "Why Emotional Intelligence Can Save Your Life?" *TalentSmartEQ*, June 20, 2022. https://www.talentsmarteq.com/emotional-intelligence-can-boost-your-career-and-save-your-life/

2. **Self-regulation** – Managing emotions so they work for you, not against you.

3. **Motivation** – Using emotional clarity to stay focused and driven

4. **Social awareness** – Understanding others' emotions and perspectives.

5. **Social regulation** – Using EQ to influence, connect, and collaborate.

These five skills apply to everyone, not just leaders. Whether you're an entry-level employee or an experienced executive, mastering EQ helps you in these areas:

- Handling feedback constructively

- Managing stress and avoiding burnout

- Building trust with colleagues and clients

- Making better decisions under pressure

CREATING A WORKPLACE WHERE EQ THRIVES

At its core, a great workplace isn't defined by policies and procedures—it's defined by its people. Organizations that invest in emotional intelligence create environments where employees thrive, teams collaborate effectively, and trust becomes a driving force behind success.

For example, take Dan, a rising leader in his company. Initially, Dan was known for his intelligence but struggled with team dynamics. He dismissed ideas quickly, got defensive during feedback, and unknowingly created a tense work environment. After focusing on improving his self-awareness and social awareness, he started adapting his communication style, reading the room better, and leading with empathy.

Over time, he became more approachable, fostered a stronger team culture, and built better relationships with his colleagues.

Contrast this with Joseph, a highly skilled but emotionally unaware manager. He lacked patience, reacted impulsively, and avoided difficult conversations. As a result, his team disengaged, and morale declined. While his technical skills remained strong, his inability to connect with his team made it difficult for him to gain support for his ideas and projects, ultimately limiting his growth within the company.

This is why EQ matters. Talent alone isn't enough. People at every level must master the human side of success.

MY EQ JOURNEY: HOW IT CHANGED MY CAREER AND RELATIONSHIPS (ADAM)

EQ isn't just something I teach—it's something that has shaped my career and my life. I took my first EQ assessment in 2010, and honestly, I didn't think much of it at the time. But as I continued to develop my self-awareness, emotional regulation, and relationship management skills, I started noticing a shift.

I became a better communicator, a better problem solver, and ultimately a better leader. But beyond my career, EQ had a profound impact on my personal life. My wife, Amber, and I have built a business together, and like any business partners, we face challenges. The ability to manage emotions, understand each other's perspectives, and communicate effectively has been a game-changer in both our personal and professional relationships.

Looking back, I can confidently say that strengthening my EQ has been one of the biggest factors in my success. And the great thing about emotional intelligence is that it's not something you're born with—it's something you can improve, just like I did.

So, where do you start? Let's dive into the steps you can take today to begin strengthening your EQ.

HOW TO START STRENGTHENING YOUR EQ TODAY

The best way to develop your EQ is to start small and build momentum. Here are a few simple strategies you can implement right now:

1. **Take your emotional temperature**: Pause for a moment and assess where you are on a scale of 1 to 10, with 1 being cool, calm, and collected, and 10 being highly emotionally charged. Pay attention to what might be triggering shifts in your emotional state—are there specific people, situations, or stressors that cause spikes? Do you notice any patterns throughout your day or week? Do certain times, environments, or circumstances tend to raise your emotional temperature? By regularly checking in and recognizing these patterns, you can begin to manage your emotions more effectively and stay in a more balanced, productive state.

2. **Pause before reacting**: When faced with a stressful situation, take a deep breath before responding. This moment of pause allows you to process your emotions, assess the situation, and choose a more thoughtful reaction, reducing the chance of an emotional outburst or miscommunication.

3. **Ask, don't assume**: Before jumping to conclusions about someone's behavior, ask clarifying questions. Seeking to understand rather than assuming intent helps prevent misunderstandings and fosters stronger relationships built on trust and mutual respect.

4. **Practice active listening**: The next time you're in a conversation, focus fully on the other person. Avoid formulating your response while they're talking. Instead, nod, paraphrase what they say, and ask follow-up questions. This shows that you value their input and strengthens your ability to connect.

5. **Identify your emotional triggers**: Pay attention to what situations or people tend to trigger strong emotions in you. Once you recognize these patterns, develop strategies to manage them, whether it's reframing your perspective, stepping away momentarily, or practicing deep breathing techniques.

6. **Identify and practice your emotional enhancers**: Just as negative triggers can cloud your emotions, emotional enhancers help clear your mental state and bring balance. Identify activities that help you reset—this could be exercise, meditation, listening to music, creative hobbies, or spending quality time with people who uplift you. Making these a regular part of your routine can help you stay emotionally resilient.

7. **Seek feedback**: Ask a trusted colleague or friend, "How do I come across in stressful situations?" Honest feedback is one of the best tools for increasing self-awareness. Be open to their insights and use them as a foundation for growth and refinement.

MAKE IT PERSONAL WITH YOUR TRIMETRIX EQ COACHING REPORT

While these strategies are a great starting point, your TriMetrix EQ Coaching Report provides an even deeper, personalized analysis. It highlights your unique strengths and areas for improvement, offering specific recommendations tailored to your emotional intelligence level. Take time to review your results and focus on the areas that will have the biggest impact on your growth.

THE ADVANTAGE OF EMOTIONAL INTELLIGENCE

Now that you understand the importance of EQ and why it's a game-changer for creating a high-performing workforce, the next step is learning how to strengthen it in real-world situations. In the next chapter, we'll dive into practical strategies that will help you further develop your EQ, apply it effectively in the workplace, and unlock new opportunities for personal and professional growth.

Are you ready to start mastering your EQ? Let's get to work.

Chapter 8 Action Items

1. **Reflect on a recent emotional reaction** at work or in a personal interaction. What emotions were present? How did they affect your response? What could you do differently next time?

2. **Commit to practicing one EQ strategy** for a week from this chapter (e.g., pausing before reacting, practicing active listening, or identifying emotional triggers) and apply it consistently in your daily interactions. Take note of any changes in your responses and outcomes.

3. **Get feedback on your EQ** by asking a trusted colleague, friend, or family member, "What's one thing I do well when it comes to handling emotions, and what's one thing I could improve?" Use this input as a starting point for growth.

4. **Review your TriMetrix EQ Coaching Report** and pick one area of EQ where you scored lower than expected. What specific recommendation does the report provide? Set a goal to improve in this area over the next 30 days.

9

Developing and Applying EQ:
Practical Strategies for Growth

Now that you understand the power of emotional intelligence (EQ), it's time to move from awareness to application. EQ allows you to take the knowledge of how emotions affect you and use it to improve your interactions, decision-making, and leadership skills.

TURNING EMOTIONAL INTELLIGENCE INTO ACTION

This chapter provides real-world strategies and frameworks to help you develop and apply EQ in ways that create immediate impact.

WORKPLACE SCENARIO: JAMES AND HIS MANAGER, OLIVIA

James is a driven and capable individual with a strong track record of success. He has consistently delivered results and is eager to take on greater responsibilities within his organization. He believes he's ready for the next level—whether that means leading a new team, expanding his responsibilities, or having greater influence within the organization.

Olivia, his manager, is an accomplished leader who has mentored many professionals throughout their careers. She sees James's potential but also recognizes that he has blind spots in his leadership style, particularly in how he communicates, handles feedback, and navigates team dynamics.

In a career development discussion, Olivia provides James with direct but constructive feedback. While he excels in technical expertise and decision-making, his emotional intelligence needs to be stronger before he's ready to take on a role with more critical responsibilities. She shares examples of where his communication has created unintended tension, how his reactions under stress impact team trust, and why advancing in his career requires more than just expertise—it requires the ability to understand and manage people effectively.

We'll explore how James processes this feedback and uses the five core skills of EQ to develop himself into a stronger leader.

OLIVIA'S PERSPECTIVE: THE ART OF CONSTRUCTIVE FEEDBACK

Olivia approached this conversation with intentionality. She knew that providing feedback on emotional intelligence could feel personal, so she framed her points as opportunities for growth. She focused on specific behaviors, avoided labeling James as "unready," and emphasized her belief in his potential. Her emotionally intelligent feedback not only motivated James but also strengthened their working relationship. She asked him to reflect on the five key EQ skills and develop a plan to make improvements.

1. SELF-AWARENESS: RECOGNIZING EMOTIONS BEFORE THEY TAKE OVER

James was caught off guard by Olivia's feedback. He had always seen himself as a strong communicator and leader, so hearing that his emotional intelligence needed improvement came as a sting. At first, he felt defensive, thinking she was undervaluing his contributions. But after taking time to reflect, he began to see the truth in her words—his quick reactions and inability to read team dynamics had held him back.

Here are a few practical steps to improve self-awareness:

- Identify emotional triggers by noting when you feel strong emotions and taking a moment to assess what caused them in real time.

- Check in with yourself: "What am I feeling right now? Why?"

- Recognize patterns in your reactions to stress, feedback, and pressure.

2. SELF-REGULATION: MANAGING EMOTIONS AND RESPONDING RATHER THAN REACTING

Instead of reacting emotionally, James took a step back and decided to observe how he handled difficult conversations. He started recognizing when frustration bubbled up and used breathing techniques to stay composed. Rather than shutting down during challenging discussions, he made a conscious effort to pause before speaking, ensuring his responses were thoughtful rather than reactive.

These practical steps can help to improve self-regulation:

- Take a moment to consider the other person's emotions and perspective before responding in a conversation.

- Focus on your emotional enhancers every day: Engage in activities that help you reset and maintain emotional clarity, such as exercise, hobbies, or connecting with supportive people.

- Develop physical habits (breathing techniques, movement) that help you stay in control.

3. MOTIVATION: USING EQ TO STAY DRIVEN AND RESILIENT

Initially, James felt discouraged. He had expected to be promoted, and Olivia's feedback felt like a roadblock. However, instead of letting this setback define him, he reframed it as an opportunity for growth. He set a personal goal to improve his emotional intelligence, seeking out mentorship, reading about leadership, and actively practicing his new skills in daily interactions.

Here are a few practical steps to improve motivation:

- Break challenges into smaller, manageable steps and focus on one positive action at a time to foster growth and learning.

- Set intrinsic goals—what personally excites you about your work?

- Develop resilience by learning from setbacks instead of dwelling on them.

4. SOCIAL AWARENESS: UNDERSTANDING OTHERS' EMOTIONS AND PERSPECTIVES

James realized that he had often focused on his performance rather than understanding how his actions affected his colleagues. One example was a recent team meeting where he had dismissed a colleague's input without realizing how deflated they felt. Recognizing this, he started paying closer attention to team interactions—reading body language, noticing shifts in energy, and asking more open-ended questions. Over time, he became more attuned to how his words and actions impacted others, leading to stronger relationships within the team.

Here are a few practical ways to improve social awareness:

- Practice active listening—focus fully on the speaker and paraphrase to confirm understanding.

- Pay attention to body language, tone, and energy in conversations.

- Ask open-ended questions to understand emotions beyond surface-level interactions.

5. SOCIAL REGULATION: MANAGING RELATIONSHIPS AND INFLUENCING EFFECTIVELY

With his new awareness and communication strategies, James made a conscious effort to foster trust and collaboration. Instead of avoiding tough conversations, he approached them with empathy and a problem-solving mindset. Over time, his team members felt more comfortable sharing their thoughts, and he was seen as a more approachable and effective leader.

These practical steps can be used to improve social regulation:

- Show understanding and acknowledge the other person's perspective before responding in difficult conversations.

- Provide constructive feedback in a way that encourages growth rather than defensiveness.

- Build strong relationships by being consistent, fair, and open to input.

James's transformation highlights the power of emotional intelligence in action. By focusing on the five factors of EQ, he became more intentional in his interactions, ultimately strengthening his relationships and effectiveness.

However, growth in EQ goes beyond learning new strategies. Applying these strategies consistently in daily interactions is the important part. Now, it's your turn to reflect on how these skills can enhance your own leadership and personal development.

REFLECTIVE QUESTIONS: APPLYING EQ TO YOUR LIFE

Consider these questions and reflect on your answers:

- Which of the five EQ skills is my greatest strength, and which needs the most improvement? (Hint: refer to your TriMetrix EQ report for this information.)

- How will improving my EQ help me achieve my personal or professional goals?

- Which relationships should I focus on first to start developing my EQ?

AVOIDING COMMON MISSTEPS

While developing EQ, it's easy to fall into common traps:

- **Overanalyzing emotions**: Spending too much time dissecting feelings without taking action may leave you stuck.

- **Avoiding feedback**: Skipping opportunities to seek input from others hinders growth.

- **Focusing only on strengths**: Ignoring areas for improvement slows progress.

By avoiding these missteps, you can maximize the impact of your efforts.

Chapter 9 Action Items

We recommend you continue to make progress on your action items from chapter 8 before taking on more. If you feel ready for more, return to your TriMetrix EQ Coaching Report and pick one additional area of EQ to work on. Set a goal to improve in this area over the next 30 days.

10

Mastering Emotional Triggers and Building Resilience

Emotional triggers are the moments when we feel our emotions spiral out of control—whether it's frustration, anger, or stress. These moments can make or break your day, influencing how you interact with others and how you make decisions. Mastering these triggers is key to building a rockstar workforce by fostering both individual and team success.

WHAT ARE EMOTIONAL TRIGGERS?

Emotional triggers often stem from situations or interactions that evoke strong reactions. At work, these might include these scenarios:

- Receiving unexpected criticism

- Dealing with last-minute changes

- Navigating conflicts with difficult coworkers

However, triggers are not limited to the workplace. They can arise in everyday life:

- Getting frustrated in bad traffic

- For parents, children not cooperating in public

- Having a disagreement with your spouse or friend

A PERSONAL EXAMPLE: THE MORNING ROUTINE BATTLE

For us, one of our biggest triggers is getting the kids out the door for school on time. The weekday morning routine can feel like a high-stakes mission, especially when we have a leadership training session first thing in the morning, knowing a group of people is waiting for us.

Our daughter in particular has made mornings a challenge. Despite our efforts—coaching her on getting out of bed on time, setting routines—some mornings feel like déjà vu, repeating the same struggles. When she wakes up late, the delay cascades into the rest of the morning, impacting everything from breakfast to the drive to school.

We used to call triggers "disablers" because they can disable our capacity to manage our emotions effectively. When the morning chaos escalates, we find ourselves raising our voices and losing patience—reactions that don't serve us or our children well.

To manage this, we've focused on proactive solutions:

- **Planning ahead**: Our daughter now picks out her outfit the night before, eliminating morning debates about wearing shorts when it's 40°F outside.

- **Removing distractions**: Coloring books are no longer allowed at the breakfast table because they slow down the process.

- **Setting realistic expectations**: We accept that some mornings will be tough, but we minimize stress by controlling what we can in advance.

Triggers can't all be avoided, but by managing what's within your control, you can minimize their impact. The lesson? Emotional clarity matters.

THE MORE YOU MANAGE YOUR INITIAL TRIGGERS,
THE BETTER YOU CAN HANDLE THE UNEXPECTED.

These events can activate the brain's "fight-or-flight" response, causing us to react impulsively. Understanding the science behind emotional hijacks helps us take back control. The amygdala, a small structure in the brain that's responsible for processing emotions, plays a key role in an emotional hijack reaction. When your brain perceives a threat—even one that isn't life-threatening, such as negative feedback—the amygdala signals an immediate response, making it harder to think clearly and respond calmly. While this instinct is useful for real danger, in everyday situations, it can lead to overreactions. Mastering your response starts with awareness and intentional practice.

Developing the ability to regulate our emotional responses not only helps us maintain personal well-being but also improves our ability to handle challenges, including conflicts. By building emotional resilience, we strengthen our ability to approach difficult conversations and stressful situations with greater clarity and control.

BUILDING EMOTIONAL RESILIENCE

Emotional resilience is the ability to bounce back from challenges and maintain composure under stress. This skill doesn't mean ignoring emotions but rather learning to process them constructively. Rockstar performers don't let stress dictate their actions; instead, they use adversity as an opportunity for growth.

REAL-LIFE EXAMPLE: TURNING A TRIGGER INTO GROWTH

Carl is a team leader who often felt overwhelmed during high-pressure meetings. During one particularly intense meeting, a disagreement with a colleague escalated, triggering Carl's frustration. He realized his emotional trigger was feeling unprepared and misunderstood in these moments. Initially, he reacted defensively, interrupting his colleague and struggling to articulate his thoughts.

Later, he reflected on the situation and identified two key EQ skills he needed to improve: self-awareness and self-regulation. Carl began practicing self-awareness by pausing to recognize his emotional state during meetings and acknowledging when he felt overwhelmed. He also worked on self-regulation by preparing key talking points ahead of time and reminding himself that it was okay not to have all the answers immediately.

Over time, Carl's ability to stay composed and thoughtfully approach disagreements improved significantly. He learned to recognize his trigger of feeling unprepared and actively worked to mitigate it through preparation and emotional regulation. This shift in managing his triggers not only enhanced his confidence but also prepared him to explore tools that help reset emotional states when triggers arise.

EMOTIONAL ENHANCERS: TOOLS TO RESET YOUR EMOTIONAL STATE

When emotional triggers occur, having tools to reset your state is crucial. Emotional enhancers are activities that help you regain control, reduce cortisol levels, and clarify your emotional state. These practices not only alleviate stress but also help you develop and apply your emotional intelligence more effectively.

EMOTIONAL ENHANCER CATEGORIES: THREE BUCKETS

To help you incorporate emotional enhancers into your daily life, consider organizing them into three categories or "buckets":

1. **Quick reset activities (five minutes or less)**. These are small actions you can take multiple times a day to reset your emotional state. Examples:

   - Deep breathing: Take a few slow, deep breaths to calm your nervous system.

   - Movement: Take a short walk or do a few stretches to release tension and re-energize your body.

   - Listen to music: Play a favorite song that helps shift your mood.

   - Sipping water or a favorite beverage: Pause to hydrate and center yourself.

2. **Regular recharge activities (30-90 minutes)**. These activities take more time but can be done several times a week to recharge your emotional energy. Examples:

   - Exercising: Go for a hike, run, hit the gym, or try yoga.

   - Spending time with loved ones: Enjoy meaningful conversations or quality time with family or friends.

   - Reading or hobbies: Dive into a book or an activity that brings you joy.

   - Nature time: Spend time outdoors to reset your perspective.

3. **Big reset activities (requires planning)**. These are larger, less frequent activities that provide a significant emotional boost. Examples:

   - Vacations: Plan a getaway to relax and recharge.

   - Road trips: Take a drive to explore new places or reconnect with nature.

- Camping: Disconnect from daily stressors and enjoy a simpler environment.

- Creative retreats: Engage in a focused activity like painting, writing, or photography.

Take a moment to consider your own emotional enhancers. What fits into each of these categories for you?

PERSONAL FAVORITES: OUR GO-TO EMOTIONAL ENHANCERS

Amber and I have found that having a few go-to emotional enhancers makes a huge difference in managing stress and staying emotionally balanced. Here are some of our personal favorites in each bucket:

QUICK RESET ACTIVITIES

- Adam: Go for a quick walk, do a few stretches, or grab an espresso.

- Amber: Stretching, a quick walk, or chatting with someone.

REGULAR RECHARGE ACTIVITIES

- Adam: Physical activity such as strength training or jiu-jitsu, and spending quality time with my wife and kids.

- Amber: Physical activity such as strength training, hiking, or Pilates, reading, and a long conversation with a close friend.

BIG RESET ACTIVITIES

- Adam: Family vacations and getaways with just Amber and me.

⚜ Amber: A spa retreat, family vacation, or engaging in something creative like vision boarding, event planning, or a flower workshop.

What about you? Reflect on which emotional enhancers work best for you and how you can integrate them into your life for ongoing balance and resilience. By identifying your go-to activities, you'll create a personal toolkit for managing stress and maintaining emotional balance.

Chapter 10 Action Items

1. **Identify your top emotional triggers**: Reflect on recent situations where you felt your emotions take over. What patterns do you notice? To help with this process, we've created an Emotional Triggers Worksheet, available in the additional resources kit accompanying this book. The worksheet guides you through identifying triggers, understanding their impact, and planning how to manage them effectively. Visit BuildingARockstarWorkforce.com to download your copy and deepen your self-awareness.

2. **Select your emotional enhancers**: Choose two or three tools from each of the three emotional enhancer categories—quick resets, regular recharge activities, and big resets—that resonate with you and fit into your daily life.

3. **Practice intentional resets**: The next time you feel triggered, use one of your chosen enhancers to regain control.

4. **Track your progress**: Keep a journal of your experiences, noting what worked and where you still feel challenged.

By understanding your emotional triggers, utilizing emotional enhancers, and building resilience, you'll be equipped to handle stress, build stronger relationships, and maintain your composure in any situation. The goal of emotional intelligence isn't perfection—it's progress.

11

Embrace the Battle:
Why You Must Lean Into Conflict

Conflict is an unavoidable reality in any workplace, team, or relationship. But rather than viewing it as something to avoid, high-performing individuals and teams recognize conflict as an opportunity for growth, collaboration, and innovation. This chapter will challenge you to rethink conflict, understand its root causes, and learn how to leverage it as a powerful leadership tool—for people at every level.

WHAT IS CONFLICT?

At its core, conflict is simply a disagreement between two or more people. But the way we perceive and respond to conflict determines whether it becomes constructive or destructive. Conflict is neither inherently good nor bad—how we manage it defines its impact.

THE TWO SIDES OF CONFLICT

In a brainstorming session, differing opinions naturally emerge. When approached constructively, team members challenge ideas with respect, refining and strengthening outcomes. However, in a dysfunctional environment, these disagreements become personal, leading to defensiveness and disengagement.

- 🛡 **Constructive conflict** leads to better solutions, strengthens relationships, and fosters innovation.

- 🛡 **Destructive conflict** breeds resentment, disengagement, and toxicity in a team or organization.

Recognizing the distinction between constructive and destructive conflict encourages teams to engage in open, transparent conversations rather than avoid difficult discussions.

CONFLICT IS NOT THE ENEMY—AVOIDING IT IS

Many individuals instinctively avoid conflict, whether in the workplace or in their personal lives. They hesitate to voice concerns, fearing backlash or discomfort. However, avoiding conflict doesn't mean it disappears—it often festers, leading to resentment, miscommunication, and larger problems down the road. Imagine an employee who disagrees with a process but stays silent, only to watch inefficiencies compound over time. Eventually, that frustration spills over, affecting the entire team's morale and productivity. This avoidance can ripple out to impact entire organizations.

Let's take this concept a step further. When we think about high-performing teams, we often imagine a seamless, harmonious environment where everyone gets along. But the reality is that the most successful teams don't avoid conflict; they navigate it effectively. In fact, we might even go so far as to say that in order to be a high-performing team, you need to have a degree of conflict—healthy conflict.

WHEN MANAGED WELL, CONFLICT STRENGTHENS RELATIONSHIPS, SHARPENS IDEAS, AND FOSTERS A CULTURE OF TRUST AND ACCOUNTABILITY.

THE ROCKSTAR WORKFORCE PERSPECTIVE

A rockstar workforce isn't built by suppressing disagreements or creating artificial harmony. It is built by embracing conflict as a tool for better outcomes. High-functioning teams and individuals view differing perspectives as opportunities.

Imagine a marketing director and a sales director in a heated discussion. Sales argues that marketing's messaging isn't driving leads, while marketing insists that sales isn't utilizing the materials correctly. At first, frustration builds and communication suffers. However, when both leaders take the time to engage in a structured conversation where they actively listen, make adjustments, and work through solutions together, they begin to find common ground. As a result, their efforts become aligned, and they develop a more effective strategy.

This situation exemplifies the Rockstar Workforce perspective on conflict. Successful teams embrace conflict as a tool for improvement rather than as a threat. By fostering openness and collaboration, teams transform disagreements into opportunities for growth and development.

How can you start looking at conflict scenarios as opportunities? Rather than obstacles, consider viewing disagreements as challenges to solve. Personally, I have made significant advancements as both an individual and a leader by shifting my mindset. Instead of focusing on the conflict itself, I look at situations through the lens of opportunity and problem-solving. This simple shift in perspective has changed how I approach difficult conversations and has made it easier for me to work through them effectively.

HEALTHY CONFLICT VERSUS UNHEALTHY CONFLICT

For a team to function at its best, conflict needs to be normal and productive. The goal isn't to eliminate conflict but to create an environment where it can be handled constructively.

These are traits of healthy conflict:

- Open and honest communication

- Respectful disagreements with a focus on problem-solving

- Encouragement of diverse perspectives

- No personal attacks or defensiveness

In contrast, these are traits of unhealthy conflict:

- Avoidance or suppression of issues

- Passive aggressiveness or gossiping

- Focus on blame rather than solutions

- Emotional outbursts and personal attacks

CONFLICT THROUGH THE LENS OF EMOTIONAL INTELLIGENCE

Remembering chapters 8 and 9 on emotional intelligence, you now know that conflict is often an emotional experience. How we handle it depends largely on our EQ skills:

- **Self-awareness**: Recognizing your triggers and responses in conflict situations.

- **Self-regulation**: Managing your emotional response to avoid knee-jerk reactions.

- **Motivation**: Identifying the motivation of each stakeholder involved in the situation.

- **Social awareness**: Understanding the emotions and perspectives of others involved.

- **Social regulation**: Guiding a conflict toward a productive resolution.

A person with high EQ recognizes when their emotional temperature is rising and takes a moment before responding. They also sense when others are in an escalated emotional state and adjust accordingly.

THE COSTS OF UNRESOLVED CONFLICT

Unaddressed conflict doesn't go away—it festers. The longer a conflict lingers, the more damage it causes to trust, morale, and productivity. Leaders who fail to manage conflict risk losing high-performing employees, damaging company culture, and creating dysfunctional teams.

Here are some common outcomes of poor conflict management:

- **Lost respect**: Employees lose trust in leaders who avoid or mishandle conflict.

- **Lack of trust**: When conflict isn't resolved, team members hesitate to speak up.

- **Damaged relationships**: Unresolved conflict creates long-term tension between individuals and teams.

- **Reduced morale**: Employees disengage when they don't feel heard.

- **High turnover**: Top talent leaves when the work environment is riddled with unaddressed conflict.

POOR CONFLICT MANAGEMENT EXAMPLE

A construction project manager overseeing a major build is under pressure to meet tight deadlines. A field superintendent notices that material deliveries are consistently late, creating inefficiencies. Concerned that these delays will cause significant disruptions, the superintendent raises the issue with the project manager. However, the manager dismisses the concerns, believing that pushing the subcontractors harder will keep the project on track. Over time, frustration builds as the delays persist. The superintendent, feeling unheard, stops raising concerns, and communication between the teams deteriorates. Deadlines are missed, quality control suffers, and costly rework becomes necessary. By the time executive leadership intervenes, the project is significantly over budget and client satisfaction has plummeted.

This scenario reflects several key outcomes as a result of unresolved conflict:

- **Lost respect**: The superintendent feels ignored, leading to disengagement.

- **Lack of trust**: The breakdown in communication erodes trust between the teams.

- **Damaged relationships**: The subcontractors and general contractors are now in conflict.

- **Reduced morale**: Workers feel frustrated and undervalued, impacting performance.

- **High turnover**: Key team members may leave due to a toxic work environment.

How could this situation have been avoided? Early intervention through active listening and collaboration could have resolved the material delay issue before it escalated. If the project manager had acknowledged the superintendent's concerns and worked with subcontractors to develop an alternative solution, the delays could have been mitigated. Regular check-ins, fostering open communication, and setting clear expectations for problem resolution are all steps that could have turned this conflict into a productive discussion rather than a costly mistake.

THE ROLE OF DISC AND BEHAVIORAL STYLES IN CONFLICT

Our natural behavioral tendencies shape how we approach and engage in conflict. Some people see conflict as a way to problem-solve, while others avoid it at all costs.

UNDERSTANDING YOUR CONFLICT STYLE

- High D (direct): Direct, assertive, and focused on results. Likely to engage in conflict head-on but may come across as abrasive.

- Low D (reflective): Reserved and cautious. May avoid conflict altogether, even when assertiveness is needed.

- High I (outgoing): People-oriented and persuasive. May avoid conflict but can use communication skills to resolve it.

- Low I (reserved): Quiet and task-focused. May withdraw from conflict or struggle to express themselves clearly.

- High S (steady): Prefers harmony and dislikes confrontation. Tends to avoid conflict, sometimes at the cost of unresolved issues.

- Low S (dynamic): More comfortable with change and quick decisions but may appear impatient or reactive in conflict.

- High C (rigorous): Detail-oriented and analytical. May engage in conflict over logic and facts but struggles with emotional elements.

- Low C (pioneering): Struggles with structure and may dismiss policies or systems during conflict.

DIFFERING CONFLICT STYLE EXAMPLE

An executive with a high D style and a high S team member disagree over a project deadline. The executive pushes aggressively for speed, while the team member values stability and process. Without understanding each other's styles, their conflict can become toxic. But with awareness, the executive can adjust their approach, and the team member can voice their concerns more confidently.

CONFLICT MANAGEMENT IS A LEADERSHIP SKILL FOR EVERYONE

Conflict management is a critical skill for everyone in an organization. A rockstar workforce is built from individuals at all levels who navigate conflict constructively, fostering trust, collaboration, and innovation.

Chapter 11 Action Items

1. **Think about the conflict management approach you used** in a recent conflict. Did you engage, avoid, or escalate the situation? What was the outcome, and how could you have handled it differently?

2. **Review the DISC conflict styles and determine where you naturally fall**. How does your approach to conflict align with your personality traits, and what adjustments can you make to improve your effectiveness in resolving disputes?

3. **Practice seeing conflict as an opportunity**. Over the next week, shift your mindset when faced with a disagreement. Instead of viewing it as a challenge, ask yourself, *How can I turn this into a productive discussion that leads to a better outcome?*

4. **Practice applying emotional intelligence in a conflict situation**. The next time conflict arises, use EQ principles—pause before reacting, assess the emotions of those involved, and guide the discussion toward a productive resolution.

5. **Engage in a constructive conflict conversation**. Identify an unresolved conflict in your workplace or personal life. Approach the conversation with openness, self-awareness, and adaptability, applying the three key objectives: recognize your approach, identify the other person's style, and adjust to best resolve the issue.

12

Turning Conflict Into Collaboration

When managed effectively, conflict can lead to stronger relationships, improved problem-solving, and a more cohesive team. The key is not to avoid conflict but to develop the skills to navigate it constructively. In this chapter, we will explore conflict resolution strategies that align with the Rockstar Workforce philosophy, ensuring leaders at all levels can turn challenges into opportunities for growth.

MANAGING CONFLICT STARTS WITH MANAGING YOURSELF

Conflict management begins with self-awareness. How you react to conflict is largely influenced by your emotions, past experiences, and stress levels.

> LEADERS WHO MANAGE THEIR EMOTIONS EFFECTIVELY CAN APPROACH CONFLICT CALMLY AND RATIONALLY, ENSURING PRODUCTIVE CONVERSATIONS RATHER THAN EMOTIONAL OUTBURSTS.

SELF-AWARENESS AND EMOTIONAL INTELLIGENCE

Emotional intelligence (EQ) plays a crucial role in conflict resolution. Self-awareness and self-regulation allow you to recognize your own biases, emotional triggers, and habitual reactions to conflict. If you are frustrated or stressed, you may react impulsively, escalating tensions rather than resolving them. Instead, you can take proactive steps to manage your emotional state before addressing conflict.

For example, imagine a manager who becomes defensive every time a team member questions their decisions. Instead of shutting down the conversation and creating frustration, a leader with strong self-awareness would recognize their emotional response, pause, and reframe the situation as an opportunity for collaboration. By controlling their initial reaction, they create a space where open discussion can lead to better solutions.

To improve self-regulation, practice these skills:

- **Pausing before responding**: Taking a deep breath or counting to three can help prevent emotional reactions.

- **Reframing the situation**: Shifting the perspective from considering it a personal attack to an opportunity for problem-solving can resolve personal differences.

- **Developing emotional agility**: Recognizing and adjusting to emotions rather than suppressing them can improve your ability to respond calmly.

- **Practicing self-reflection**: Journaling or reviewing past conflicts can reveal response patterns and areas for improvement.

Before we dive into different approaches to conflict, take a moment to evaluate how you currently handle conflict using the self-assessment below. Each question highlights a key skill, and every response can be translated into an actionable strategy for improvement.

CONFLICT MANAGEMENT ASSESSMENT

		DISAGREE									AGREE
1	You readily identify and address issues, concerns or conflicts.	1	2	3	4	5	6	7	8	9	10
2	You recognize opportunities for positive outcomes in conflict situations.	1	2	3	4	5	6	7	8	9	10
3	You read situations accurately to pinpoint critical issues.	1	2	3	4	5	6	7	8	9	10
4	You actively listen to gain understanding of issues from different perspectives.	1	2	3	4	5	6	7	8	9	10
5	You diffuse tension and effectively handle emotional situations.	1	2	3	4	5	6	7	8	9	10
6	You assist people with opposing views or opinions to identify common interests.	1	2	3	4	5	6	7	8	9	10
7	You strive to settle differences in a fair manner.	1	2	3	4	5	6	7	8	9	10
8	You settle differences without damaging relationships.	1	2	3	4	5	6	7	8	9	10
9	You strive to limit the negative aspects of conflict while increasing the positive.	1	2	3	4	5	6	7	8	9	10
10	You focus on enhancing learning and group outcomes when solving conflict.	1	2	3	4	5	6	7	8	9	10

YOUR SCORE

What area(s) do you need to focus on most?

Conflict is inevitable, but how we manage it makes all the difference. This self-assessment helps you reflect on your current approach to conflict and identify areas where you can improve. The following insights offer a deeper understanding of why these skills matter and provide practical steps to strengthen your ability to navigate conflict effectively. Use this section as a guide to refine your conflict management approach and turn challenges into opportunities for growth and collaboration.

CONFLICT MANAGEMENT NEXT STEPS

1. **Readily identifies and addresses issues, concerns, or conflicts.**

   Many people avoid addressing conflict out of fear of making things worse, but avoidance only allows tension to grow. Those who handle conflict well tend to lean into difficult conversations with confidence.

   How to improve: The next time you feel hesitant to address an issue, remind yourself that early action leads to faster resolutions and stronger relationships.

2. **Recognizes opportunities for positive outcomes in conflict situations.**

   Seeing conflict as negative can limit your ability to lead effectively. Conflict sparks innovation and builds deeper trust when handled correctly.

   How to improve: Challenge yourself to reframe conflict. Each disagreement is a chance to strengthen communication and find creative solutions.

3. **Reads situations accurately to pinpoint critical issues.**

   Jumping to conclusions in a conflict can create misunderstandings and frustration. The ability to analyze a situation before reacting ensures a thoughtful and effective response.

   How to improve: Before offering a solution, ask yourself, *Am I addressing the real issue, or just the surface-level problem?*

4. **Actively listens to gain understanding of an issue from different perspectives.**

Many people listen to respond, not to understand—this can escalate conflict instead of resolving it. Active listening builds trust and leads to stronger solutions.

How to improve: When in a discussion, focus fully on the speaker. Summarize their perspective before responding to ensure you truly understand their point of view.

5. **Diffuses tension and effectively handles emotional situations.**

Emotions can run high during conflict, and if they aren't managed, they can derail productive discussions. Leaders who stay calm help others do the same.

How to improve: If tension rises, take a deep breath and slow down the conversation. Acknowledge emotions but steer the focus toward solutions rather than blame.

6. **Assists people with opposing views or opinions to identify common interests.**

When people are at odds, they often focus only on their differences, making resolution seem impossible. Helping others find common ground builds collaboration.

How to improve: In a conflict, ask both sides, "What do we agree on?" Identifying shared goals shifts the conversation from opposition to teamwork.

7. **Strives to settle differences in a fair manner.**

Unfair conflict resolution can create resentment and disengagement. Leaders who prioritize fairness ensure that all perspectives are heard and considered.

How to improve: Before making a decision, ask yourself, *Am I considering all viewpoints, or am I favoring one side?* Strive for a resolution that benefits the greater good.

8. **Settles differences without damaging relationships.**

Winning an argument at the expense of a relationship can lead to long-term issues. Effective conflict resolution strengthens, rather than weakens, connections.

How to improve: Approach every conflict with respect. Even when disagreeing, show appreciation for the other person's perspective to maintain trust and collaboration.

9. **Strives to limit the negative aspects of conflict while increasing the positive.**

Conflict can either be destructive or constructive, depending on how it's handled. Focusing only on the negatives makes conflict feel like a threat rather than an opportunity.

How to improve: Shift your mindset—view conflict as a tool for growth. Ask yourself, *How can this situation make our relationship stronger?*

10. **Focuses on enhancing learning and group outcomes when resolving conflict.**

Conflict should be about more than just settling disputes. It should improve team dynamics and problem-solving skills. Leaders who foster learning create stronger teams.

How to improve: After resolving a conflict, take a moment to reflect. Ask, "What did we learn from this, and how can we improve for the future?"

Mastering conflict management doesn't mean eliminating disagreements—it turns them into opportunities to strengthen relationships, foster trust, and drive better outcomes. By developing these skills, you not only enhance your leadership effectiveness but also contribute to a healthier, more productive work environment. The next time conflict arises, view it as an opportunity to apply what you've learned and create positive change.

THE FIVE APPROACHES TO CONFLICT (THOMAS-KILMANN MODEL)

Conflict resolution is not one-size-fits-all. Depending on the situation, different approaches may be more effective. Below, we expand on each of the five approaches identified within the Thomas-Kilmann model, to help you understand when and how to apply them effectively.

1. **Competing (I win, you lose)**: Used when quick, decisive action is necessary. Works best in high-stakes situations where time is limited.

    Example: During a heated team meeting, a manager steps in and shuts down a conversation before it escalates further.

    Potential pitfall: Overuse of this approach can make others feel unheard or undervalued.

    When to use: When preventing damage or maintaining control is more important than consensus.

2. **Collaborating (win-win)**: The ideal strategy for fostering innovation and strengthening relationships. This approach seeks mutually beneficial solutions where both parties feel satisfied with the outcome.

Example: A cross-functional team working together to create a new product strategy, ensuring that marketing, engineering, and sales all contribute and benefit from the solution.

Potential pitfall: Can be time-consuming if not managed efficiently.

When to use: When building strong, long-term relationships is a priority and creative solutions are possible.

3. **Compromising (meet in the middle)**: A balance between assertiveness and cooperation, often used when both parties need to give up something. This approach is useful when both parties are willing to give a little. It can also be quick and efficient if the parties have built trust.

    Example: Two department heads agreeing to share a budget increase instead of one getting full funding.

    Potential pitfall: Can lead to suboptimal outcomes if both parties sacrifice too much.

    When to use: When both sides hold equal power, and a quick resolution is needed.

4. **Avoiding (Conflict? What conflict?)**: Useful when the issue is minor or when more information is needed before engaging. This approach can help diffuse tension in emotionally charged situations by allowing time for emotions to settle.

    Example: A team leader postponing a discussion about minor workflow disagreements to focus on immediate deadlines.

    Potential pitfall: Avoiding conflict for too long can allow problems to fester and grow.

When to Use: When the conflict is trivial, emotions are too high, or addressing it at a later time will lead to better outcomes.

5. **Accommodating (you win, I lose)**: Prioritizing relationships over personal gains, effective when maintaining harmony is more important than the issue at hand.

Example: A project manager agreeing to a team member's preferred approach to maintain goodwill and team morale.

Potential pitfall: Can lead to resentment if used too often or when personal needs are consistently overlooked.

When to use: When the issue is minor and preserving the relationship is more important than the specific outcome.

SELF-REFLECTION EXERCISE

Take a moment to reflect on how you typically handle conflict. Do you tend to favor one approach over others? While having a preferred style is natural, effective conflict management often requires flexibility. Consider whether there are other approaches you could use more frequently to achieve better outcomes.

Try this: Think of a recent conflict you've faced. Did you use the most effective approach for the situation? How might a different approach have changed the outcome?

As you continue reading, we will explore how identifying the root causes of conflict can further enhance your ability to navigate these situations effectively.

IDENTIFYING THE ROOT CAUSES OF CONFLICT

Picture this: Two colleagues, once enthusiastic about collaborating, now avoid each other entirely. What started as a simple miscommunication about project priorities has snowballed into resentment, affecting team morale and productivity. Neither party truly understands what went wrong, only that they no longer trust each other. Believe it or not, these types of situations can quickly escalate and spiral out of control.

Understanding the root cause of conflict helps address the core issue rather than just the symptoms. One effective method for uncovering the underlying cause of conflict is the Five Whys method. This technique involves asking *why* multiple times to dig deeper into the root of an issue, rather than stopping at surface-level explanations.

For example:

1. **Why did the project deadline get missed?** The team misunderstood the scope.

2. **Why was the scope misunderstood?** The client's expectations were not clearly communicated.

3. **Why were expectations unclear?** The project manager assumed they were understood but didn't confirm.

4. **Why didn't the project manager confirm expectations?** They were focused on meeting another deadline.

5. **Why were they juggling multiple deadlines?** Resource allocation was not properly managed.

By repeatedly asking *why*, you can trace conflict back to its origins and develop solutions that address the real issue, rather than just the symptoms.

As you move forward, take a moment to think about a recent conflict you've experienced. Could asking *why* multiple times have helped reveal deeper insights into what really caused it? Understanding these underlying issues is the first step toward meaningful conflict resolution.

To better understand workplace conflict, it's helpful to recognize the common sources that contribute to tension and disputes. Below are some of the most frequent causes of conflict and how they can impact team dynamics.

- **Miscommunication**: Many conflicts arise from misunderstandings. Tying back to dynamic communication, you must ensure clarity in your messaging.

- **Competing values**: Employees with different priorities or motivations may struggle to align their approaches, as highlighted in the Driving Forces framework.

- **Personality clashes**: Your TriMetrix EQ Coaching Report highlights how your behavioral style interacts with others. Differing work styles can lead to misunderstandings and friction, but recognizing these tendencies helps you adapt and collaborate more effectively.

- **Lack of trust**: When trust is low, assumptions and misunderstandings increase, creating unnecessary conflict. Rebuilding trust doesn't take grand gestures—just steady, reliable actions over time.

Now that you have a framework for identifying the root causes of conflict, let's explore a structured approach for resolving these issues effectively, using the five-step conflict resolution process.

THE FIVE-STEP CONFLICT RESOLUTION PROCESS

Conflict resolution requires a structured approach to ensure that issues are addressed effectively and lead to positive outcomes. By following these five steps, you can navigate conflicts in a way that strengthens relationships and fosters understanding.

1. ADDRESS CONFLICT EARLY

- The longer a conflict lingers, the more resentment and frustration can build. Addressing the issue early prevents it from escalating into a bigger problem.

- Avoiding conflict may seem like the easier option, but unresolved issues often resurface in unexpected ways.

- Proactive tip: Recognize the early warning signs of conflict, such as miscommunication, passive-aggressive behavior, or decreased collaboration.

2. LISTEN FIRST, SPEAK SECOND

- Effective conflict resolution starts with listening. When people feel heard, they are more open to finding solutions.

- Listen to understand, not to respond. Ask clarifying questions and acknowledge the other person's perspective before offering your input.

- Proactive tip: Use active listening techniques—maintain eye contact, paraphrase what the other person said, and avoid interrupting.

3. FOCUS ON THE PROBLEM, NOT THE PERSON

- Conflict often becomes personal when emotions take over. It's crucial to separate the issue from the individual to maintain a constructive conversation.

- Instead of placing blame, frame the conversation around solving the problem together.

- Proactive tip: Use "I" statements instead of "You" statements (e.g., "I feel that our communication needs improvement" versus "You never communicate with me").

4. FIND COMMON GROUND

- Resolution comes from working together, not against each other. Identify shared goals and areas of agreement.

- When both parties focus on their common interests rather than their differences, they are more likely to reach a mutually beneficial outcome.

- Proactive tip: Ask, "What is one thing we both agree on?" to shift the mindset toward collaboration.

5. CONFIRM THE RESOLUTION

- Once an agreement is reached, confirm the next steps and expectations. This prevents further misunderstandings.

- Summarize the resolution to ensure both parties are on the same page.

- Proactive tip: End with a positive reinforcement—acknowledge the effort both sides made to find a resolution.

SCENARIO: A CUSTOMER SERVICE REPRESENTATIVE RESOLVES A CONFLICT USING THE FIVE STEPS

A frustrated customer calls a company's support line, upset about an unexpected charge on their invoice. The customer service representative (CSR) uses the five-step conflict resolution process to handle the situation.

STEP 1: ADDRESS CONFLICT EARLY

Instead of dismissing the complaint or deflecting responsibility, the CSR acknowledges the customer's frustration and expresses a willingness to resolve the issue.

STEP 2: LISTEN FIRST, SPEAK SECOND

The CSR patiently listens as the customer explains their frustration. They avoid interrupting and ask clarifying questions to ensure they fully understand the issue.

STEP 3: FOCUS ON THE PROBLEM, NOT THE PERSON

Rather than saying, "You didn't read the terms correctly," the CSR rephrases: "I understand how frustrating this charge must feel. Let's look into why it was applied and see what we can do about it."

STEP 4: FIND COMMON GROUND

The CSR identifies that both the customer and the company want a fair resolution. They acknowledge that the customer was unaware of the charge and offer possible solutions, such as a partial refund or a service credit.

STEP 5: CONFIRM THE RESOLUTION

After agreeing on a service credit, the CSR restates the resolution: "Just to confirm, we're applying a $20 service credit to your account, and I've sent you a confirmation email with all the details. I appreciate your patience in resolving this today."

By following these steps, the CSR not only diffuses the situation but also strengthens the customer's trust in the company.

CONFLICT AS A CATALYST FOR GROWTH

Throughout this chapter, you've learned how self-awareness, emotional intelligence, and structured conflict resolution strategies can transform disagreements into productive discussions. Whether you're choosing the right conflict approach, identifying root causes, or using the five-step resolution process, these skills will help you master conflict in any situation.

CONFLICT ISN'T SOMETHING TO FEAR—
IT'S AN OPPORTUNITY FOR GROWTH.

A rockstar workforce doesn't eliminate conflict; it masters it. The most effective leaders build trust, improve teamwork, and strengthen their organizations by embracing conflict as a natural and necessary process.

Chapter 12 Action Items

1. **Identify your natural conflict-handling style** using insights from DISC and EQ.

2. **Observe a conflict at work** this week. What approaches were used? Did they resolve the issue effectively, or could a different approach have been better? Take notes and reflect on how you might have handled it differently.

3. **Practice using one of the five conflict resolution techniques** in a conversation this week.

4. Before the end of today, **reflect on a recent conflict you've experienced** and identify which conflict-handling approach you used. Was it the most effective choice? If not, how could you have approached it differently?

5. **Use a conflict as a leadership opportunity** to strengthen a relationship.

By mastering conflict, leaders and employees alike will be equipped to foster a culture of trust, collaboration, and high performance. Conflict, when handled correctly, is not a roadblock—it's a stepping stone toward building a rockstar workforce.

13

Beyond the Book:
How to Make Leadership Stick for Everyone

Leadership isn't about a title or position—it's a mindset. The most successful leaders understand that growth never stops. Like elite athletes who constantly train, refine their skills, and adapt to new competition, great leaders continuously invest in their development. This mindset is what separates good leaders from great ones—those who embrace challenges, stay curious, and commit to elevating those around them.

THE ROCKSTAR MINDSET: LEADERSHIP AS A LIFELONG JOURNEY

Think back to Jordan from the introduction, the employee who took initiative to resolve a communication breakdown. What made Jordan different from Alex, who avoided addressing the issue? It wasn't a title or years of experience. It was a mindset—a willingness to step up, take ownership, and create positive change. Leaders don't wait for permission; they take action.

A rockstar mindset is built on three key principles:

1. **Continuous learning**: Never assume you've arrived. Stay curious, seek feedback, and push yourself to grow.

2. **Adaptability**: The world is constantly evolving. People who embrace change rather than resist it will always stay ahead.

3. **Resilience**: Challenges are inevitable. How you respond to setbacks defines your ability to lead.

BUILDING A ROCKSTAR WORKFORCE CULTURE

Developing a rockstar workforce requires creating a culture where leadership is woven into daily operations. When organizations invest in developing people at every level, they unlock the full potential of their workforce.

Consider Richard and Erik's story from chapter 1. Their decision to invest in leadership development for their entire company—rather than just the management team—transformed the business. Employees in every position became more engaged, took greater ownership, and collaborated more effectively. It wasn't about teaching managers how to manage; it was about teaching **everyone** how to lead.

Creating this kind of culture starts with three key areas:

- **Hiring and onboarding**: Look beyond technical skills—hire for leadership potential. From day one, reinforce that leadership isn't about titles but about action.

- **Ongoing development**: Leadership isn't learned in a single workshop. Embed continuous learning through development programs, mentorship, coaching, training, and peer-to-peer collaboration.

- **Accountability and recognition**: Celebrate leadership behaviors. When employees take initiative, solve problems, and elevate others, recognize and reward those actions.

MEASURING SUCCESS AND ENSURING LONG-TERM IMPACT

How do you know if your leadership culture is working? Beyond financial performance, organizations that commit to developing leaders see tangible benefits: higher employee engagement, lower turnover, and a more resilient workforce.

Justin's company, featured in chapter 1, saw massive growth when they shifted from developing only senior leaders to developing **everyone**. Employees became more adaptable, cross-functional collaboration improved, and the company's growth skyrocketed. These changes didn't happen by accident—they happened because leadership development became a strategic priority.

To ensure long-term impact, organizations should incorporate these practices into normal operations:

- Regularly assess leadership engagement and development.

- Use 360-degree feedback (covered in chapter 2) to measure leadership behaviors at all levels.

- Foster a culture where leadership discussions happen in every team meeting, not just in executive boardrooms.

A CALL TO ACTION: YOUR NEXT STEPS

The question now is—what will you do with what you've learned?

> LEADERSHIP DEVELOPMENT DOESN'T END WITH
> READING A BOOK OR ATTENDING A WORKSHOP.

Strengthening your leadership requires consistent action. Whether you're an individual contributor or a CEO, you have the power to elevate yourself and those around you.

We challenge you to commit to your leadership growth:

- **For individuals**: Revisit the action items from previous chapters and prioritize the ones that align most with your current growth areas. Visit the book's website at

BuildingARockstarWorkforce.com to access additional resources that will support your development.

🛡 **For organizations**: Identify ways to integrate leadership development into your culture. It could be launching a Rockstar Workforce development series, revisiting your hiring practices, implementing a mentoring program, or creating other opportunities for employees to grow.

As you move forward, remember this: Leadership isn't about a title. It's about impact. It's about creating an environment where **everyone** can step up, contribute, and grow.

You have everything you need to build the foundation of a rockstar workforce. Now, it's time to take action.

Acknowledgments

Writing *Building a Rockstar Workforce* has been one of the most meaningful projects we've ever taken on. It stretched us, challenged us, and gave us the opportunity to reflect deeply on the work we do every day. More than a book, this is a tribute to the incredible people we've worked with—thank you for your help in shaping the ideas and lessons inside.

To our clients and the Rockstar Workforce community—thank you for trusting us to help grow your people and your teams. So many of the lessons and stories in this book come directly from the work we've done together. You've inspired us more than you know.

To the amazing team at Aloha Publishing—Jennifer Regner, Beth Berger, Heather Goetter, and Maryanna Young—we can't thank you enough. You helped us shape our ideas into a real book and guided us with patience, clarity, and encouragement the whole way through.

To the many mentors and peers who have poured into us over the years—thank you for your wisdom, perspective, and encouragement. Whether it was a quick word of advice, a generous share of your experience, or just being someone we could learn from, your influence has helped shape our thinking and this book.

To our partners at TTI Success Insights—thank you for creating the book contest that kicked all this off. It was the spark we didn't know we needed. We're especially grateful for the friendships, mentors, and brilliant minds we've been able to learn from in the TTI community over the years. You've influenced not just this book, but how we serve our clients every day.

To you, the reader—thank you for investing in your own growth. We hope this book helps you lead with more confidence, clarity, and connection. You're exactly the kind of person this book was written for.

And of course—to Hudson and Harper. You two are the heart behind everything we do. Thanks for cheering us on (even when you had no idea what we were working on), for being patient during the long working sessions, and for reminding us that leadership starts at home—with love, laughter, and a whole lot of snack breaks.

And above all, to each other—this book is one more example of what we can build together. Marriage, business, parenting, writing . . . none of it's easy, but there's no one else we'd rather have for a partner.

—Adam & Amber

About the Authors

Adam and Amber Wong are a husband-and-wife team who bring a combined 25-plus years of leadership and business experience to the work they love—helping people grow. As the founders of Rockstar Workforce, they've coached, trained, and partnered with organizations of all shapes and sizes to build high-performing teams from the inside out.

Their signature approach—what they call *Leadership Mechanics™*—focuses on practical, real-world ways to develop leadership skills that actually stick. They believe that leadership isn't just for people with titles. Everyone, at every level, has the potential to lead.

Amber holds a B.A. from Arizona State University. Adam earned his MBA from Grand Canyon University and his B.A. from Northern Arizona University. They're also proud parents of Hudson and Harper, and when they're not working with leaders, you'll find them chasing kids, practicing jiu-jitsu (Adam), or sneaking in a coffee date between meetings.

Together, they're on a mission to make leadership development more human, more actionable, and more fun.

About Rockstar Workforce

Rockstar Workforce is a leadership development company founded by Adam and Amber Wong, built on the belief that everyone has the potential to lead—regardless of their title. We help organizations transform their cultures and results by developing leaders at every level.

Through years of real-world experience, we've seen firsthand what works and what doesn't when it comes to people development. That's why our programs aren't built on theory alone. They're packed with practical tools, relatable language, and powerful insights grounded in behavioral science and emotional intelligence.

Whether you're a business leader working to invest in your people, an HR or L&D professional searching for a meaningful leadership solution, or an individual ready to grow—we're here to help you build the skills that move the needle.

Our signature three-part leadership program includes:

1. **Foundations** – Develop self-awareness, dynamic communication, emotional intelligence, and conflict management skills.

2. **Performance** – Build habits for setting and achieving goals, strategic thinking, managing stress, and personal productivity.

3. **Results** – Strengthen accountability, improve coaching, elevate delegation, and foster high-performing teams.

At Rockstar Workforce, we teach what we live. We keep it real. We keep it human. And we give people the tools they need to lead with clarity, confidence, and heart.

Let's Stay Connected

If you've made it to this page, it means you're serious about becoming a stronger, more impactful leader—and we're here for it. One of the best parts of this work is getting to stay in touch with the amazing people who pick up this book and put these tools into action.

We'd love to keep the conversation going and continue supporting your growth. Whether you're looking for practical tools, extra resources, leadership insights, or a little motivation, we've got something for you.

Below and on the next page are all the places you can connect with us, follow along, and find what you need, when you need it.

Book website: www.BuildingARockstarWorkforce.com
Company website: www.RockstarWorkforce.com

in Linkedin: (company) www.linkedin.com/company/rockstarworkforce
(Adam) www.linkedin.com/in/adamwong-rockstarworkforce/
(Amber) www.linkedin.com/in/amberlwong/

O Instagram: (company) @RockstarWorkforce
(Adam) @AdamWongAZ
(Amber) @AmberWongAZ

f Facebook: (company) www.facebook.com/RockstarWorkforce/

YouTube: (company) www.youtube.com/@rockstarworkforce

Threads: (company) @RockstarWorkforce
(Adam) @Adamwongaz

SCAN ME

BEFORE YOU GO

Thanks again for being part of this journey. If you haven't already, make sure to grab our downloadable tools from BuildingARockstarWorkforce.com—they're designed to help you apply what you've learned and make this stick. And if something from the book resonated with you, let us know! We love hearing what stood out and how you're using it.

Keep leading. Keep growing. And let's keep in touch.

—Adam & Amber

LEADERSHIP DEVELOPMENT DOESN'T END WITH
READING A BOOK OR ATTENDING A WORKSHOP.

Rockstar

WORKFORCE

www.ingramcontent.com/pod-product-compliance
Lightning Source LLC
Chambersburg PA
CBHW050507210326
41521CB00011B/2362